Reading Activities

Reading Activities for Today's Elementary Schools

Paul C. Burns
Late of the University of Tennessee

Betty D. Roe
Tennessee Technological University

UNIVERSITY
PRESS OF
AMERICA

Lanham • New York • London

Library of Congress Cataloging-in-Publication Data

Burns, Paul Clay, 1923-
Reading activities for today's elementary
schools/Paul C. Burns, Betty D. Roe.
p. cm.
Reprint. Previously published: Boston :
Houghton Mifflin, © 1979.
Includes bibliographical references and index.
1. Reading (Elementary)   2. Reading games.
3. Education, Elementary—Activity programs.
I. Roe, Betty D.   II. Title.
LB1573.B8817   1991
372.4'1—dc20   91–7352 CIP

ISBN 0–8191–8055–6 (pbk.)

 The paper used in this publication meets the minimum requirements of
American National Standard for Information Sciences—Permanence
of Paper for Printed Library Materials, ANSI Z39.48–1984.

Dedicated to
Carrie Lee Cartee Burns
and Josephine Moorhead Daniel

contents

three

Pre-reading Experiences 40

four

Word Recognition 59

five

Vocabulary and Comprehension 78

six

Study Skills 106

seven

Content-Area Reading 123

eight

Literary Appreciation—Prose and Poetry 142

nine

Oral Reading and Drama 160

ten

Recreational and Informational Reading 177

Preface

This book of reading activities is designed for use in classrooms where stimulating programs require that a variety of materials be used within the learning environment. It will be helpful as a resource text in undergraduate and graduate reading classes and also as reference book for in-service teachers.

The activities have been developed to correspond with the major reading concepts and tasks. They can be helpful in providing interesting and purposeful reinforcement to a wide variety of basic reading skills. They can serve as resources for ideas and as models for varying extensions of the ideas. Many of the activities promote independent work and divergent thinking, while others can be used with the entire class or small groups. They develop and strengthen a linguistic base for reading. The activities take into account a wide range of achievement levels. They are a collection of practical things to do in the classroom, each of which should be selected by the teacher based on the pupils' needs and then strengthened and illumined by the teacher's imagination in using it with children.

The authors hope you will find the activities useful, logically organized, and presented in a clear format. The appendices should serve as ready references, as can the other lists of resources provided throughout the text.

The authors wish to acknowledge deep appreciation to the following persons who read the original manuscript and contributed many helpful suggestions: Maribeth Henny, Department of Elementary Education of Iowa State University, Ames, Iowa; H. D. Jacobs, Reading Clinic Coordinator, College of Education, Arizona State University, Tempe, Arizona; and Ivan J. Quandt, College of Education, Temple University, Philadelphia, Pennsylvania.

Paul C. Burns
University of Tenessee at Knoxville

Betty D. Roe
Tennessee Technological University
Cookeville

one

Introduction

VOLUME AND CHAPTER ORGANIZATION

As noted in the table of contents, this book contains ten chapters, plus appendices. The first two chapters are general: Chapter 1 describes the contents of this book and how to use it, and Chapter 2 describes some basic teacher-made and collected materials that will be helpful in any reading program.

Chapters 3 through 9 focus on specific skill areas: pre-reading experiences, word recognition, comprehension, study skills, content areas (social studies, science, math, etc.), literature, and oral reading and drama. Chapter 10 contains activities to promote special interests—recreational reading ideas. The appendices contain other useful items: (a) easy reading book series; (b) multi-level instructional materials; (c) sources of free and inexpensive teaching materials; (d) publishers' addresses.

Chapters 3 through 10 are organized in the following manner: Each specific chapter begins with a short background section, which explains the area and the component parts that are treated. For easy reference and for cross-indexing of activities, each activity is numbered and includes the following features:

1. Objective—telling what the student will learn from participating in the activity.
2. Materials needed/diagrams—indicating the common materials needed, often accompanied by diagrams to indicate clearly what is required to do the activity.
3. Directions—stating the procedures to be used with the activity.
4. Designation of level—suggesting major levels [either primary (K–3) or intermediate (4–8)] at which activities work best, although they may be useful at any level.

GUIDELINES FOR READING ACTIVITIES

In preparing the activities and games for this volume, the following guidelines have been used:

1. The activity or game develops or reinforces important instructional objectives.
2. Many of the activities are planned so they may be done by several children without the need for teacher direction once basic instructions have been given.
3. Self-correction features are incorporated in many activities to help reduce demands upon the teacher's time and to provide immediate feedback.
4. The format is interesting to children. Each activity has intrinsic interest. These are not just disguised practice exercises.
5. Each activity stands on its own, and each activity contains enough material so students will find it interesting as well as helpful in learning important skills.
6. Each activity accomplishes one or more of the following:
   a. Creates a learning situation where the fundamental concept or skill is being practiced in the process of participation.
   b. Rewards players on a team for cooperative effort.
   c. Provides an opportunity for the children themselves to serve as models for other children.
   d. Requires a strategy that forces the participants to learn or practice the reading concept featured.
   e. Causes the participants to be active participants.

7. The activity produces measurable effects on those that participate in it.

The teacher who wishes to create or to select commercial activities to supplement those in this book will find the following ideas helpful:

1. First, and of major importance, decide what objective an activity is expected to accomplish. Any activity chosen should be designed to aid in the accomplishment of one or more of the objectives of a reading program.
2. Carefully review the list of guidelines for an activity on page 2 and try to develop or choose an activity that elicits a positive response to each of the guidelines.
3. Consider the various types of activities that might be used.
4. Consider the interests of the children. For example, if many boys and girls are interested in hockey, then a hockey-related activity or game would probably create interest.
5. Make a mock-up of the activity, and try it out with several children as a means of refining it.
6. Develop a set of instructions. Have a group of children try to participate in the activity using only the mock-up and the instructions. If the children are at the pre-reading level, use a cassette tape to convey the instructions.
7. Refine the activity and the instructions on the basis of the try-out suggested in point 6.

USING READING ACTIVITIES

Under desirable circumstances, teachers can use reading activities and games to good advantage. Such activities can be used not only to introduce interest and excitement into a learning program, but also to help a child attain a wide range of competencies. The following list of reasons for the use of activity strategies in the classroom suggests some of their functions. Activities can:

• Be used successfully with children who have a reading deficiency.
• Be used to help with management problems that occur when a child is bored with the regular classroom routine.
• Fit well into the classroom where the learning center approach is used.
• Provide students with an opportunity to vary from being passive consumers of information to being active decision makers.

• Promote desirable social interactions among children by encouraging cooperation and discussion.

• Provide an opportunity to integrate reading with other subjects.

• Be geared to conform to the particular interests of students.

• Provide the teacher with diagnostic information that can be used to help individual children correct misconceptions or fill gaps in their learning structures.

The authors urge the reader to become familiar with the activities before using this book in a classroom. As you observe your pupils at work, note weak areas of skill development. Check any activities that may fit the needs of a particular child or group of children. In using an activity with a child, let him or her know how an activity or game will help.

Any of the following organizational combinations may be effectively used with the activities:

1. During the work time of a lesson with a group of children, others may engage in a variety of skill activities.

2. After diagnostic tests, the entire class may engage in various activities. Some of the children can be working on skills that need further reinforcement, and those who had few problem areas can be engaged in enrichment activities.

3. As an introduction to a new skill, the entire class might be engaged in a developmental activity or, more likely, the class could be broken into five or six groups, with each group involved in the same activity.

4. A teacher might suggest particular activities to class members who need additional skill practice. These activities could be used during a child's free time or taken home to be used with a friend, sibling, or parent.

Some words of caution and advice are important concerning the use of activities such as those presented in this and other sourcebooks.

Informal skill tests should be utilized to help the teacher determine the specific skill needs of the students. Use a simple skill test or a checklist designed to measure the child's accomplishment of some particular reading skill. The results can be used to determine whether or not the child needs instruction in a particular skill. The following types of skill tests, for example, could be utilized for the word-recognition activities presented in this book:

Sight words: Any basic list of sight words, such as Dolch Sight Words.

GRAPH FOR ESTIMATING READABILITY — EXTENDED

by Edward Fry, Rutgers University Reading Center, New Brunswick, N.J. 08904

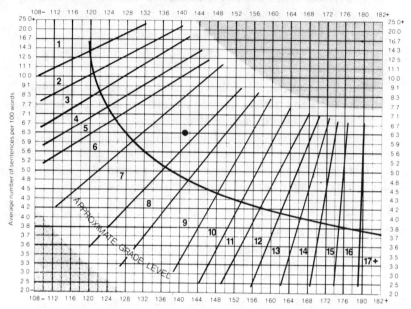

Expanded Directions for Working Readability Graph

1. Randomly select three (3) sample passages and count out exactly 100 words each, beginning with the beginning of a sentence. Do count proper nouns, initializations, and numerals.
2. Count the number of sentences in the hundred words, estimating length of the fraction of the last sentence to the nearest one-tenth.
3. Count the total number of syllables in the 100-word passage. If you don't have a hand counter available, an easy way is to simply put a mark above every syllable over one in each word, then when you get to the end of the passage, count the number of marks and add 100. Small calculators can also be used as counters by pushing numeral 1, then push the + sign for each word or syllable when counting.
4. Enter graph with *average* sentence length and *average* number of syllables; plot dot where the two lines intersect. Area where dot is plotted will give you the approximate grade level.
5. If a great deal of variability is found in syllable count or sentence count, putting more samples into the average is desirable.
6. A word is defined as a group of symbols with a space on either side; thus, *Joe, IRA, 1945,* and & are each one word.
7. A syllable is defined as a phonetic syllable. Generally, there are as many syllables as vowel sounds. For example, *stopped* is one syllable and *wanted* is two syllables. When counting syllables for numerals and initializations, count one syllable for each symbol. For example, *1945* is four syllables, *IRA* is three syllables, and & is one syllable.

Note: This "extended graph" does not outmode or render the earlier (1968) version inoperative or inaccurate; it is an extension. (REPRODUCTION PERMITTED—NO COPYRIGHT)

Context clues: Activity No. 4.3 on page 64 can serve as an informal skill test if the material is at the child's instructional level. Check the readability by using *Fry's Graph for Estimating Readability* (see page 5) or any commonly used readability formula.

Phonics: Measures the child's knowledge of single consonant sounds, vowel sounds, consonant blends, and consonant digraphs.

Structural analysis: Measures the child's knowledge of common prefixes and suffixes, common inflectional endings, contractions, compound words, syllabication.

Dictionary: Measures the child's knowledge of syllabication and accent.

Here is one sample skills test for checking a child's knowledge of the hard and soft c. It might be used previous to Activity #4.10.

Skill Test: Hard and soft sound of c

Place a checkmark beside the words that contain a soft c sound (as in celery).

____ can	____ car	____ came
____ cent	____ city	____ cell
____ cider	____ cat	____ circus

Place a checkmark beside the words that begin with a hard c sound (as in cat).

____ cow	____ cycle	____ cup
____ cut	____ cat	____ cereal
____ circle	____ cob	____ cold

Initial instruction is needed prior to the use of the activities, as they are intended largely for practice and reinforcement. A sample lesson plan for teaching the soft sound of c is provided below. (A similar lesson or lessons would be provided for the hard sound of c.)

Teaching Plan

Write on the chalkboard the following words, all of which the children have learned previously as sight words:

cent	cereal
city	cymbol
circle	cider

Ask the children to listen carefully as the written words are pronounced. Ask the class: "Did any parts of these words sound the same?" If an affirmative reply is received, ask, "What parts sound the same?" This should elicit the answer that the first sound in each word was the same or that the words sounded alike at the beginning.

Next ask the children to look carefully at the words written on the board. Then ask, "Do you see anything that is the same in all these words?" This should elicit the answer that all of the words have the same first letter or all the words start with c̲.

Ask what the children can conclude about certain words that begin with the letter c̲. The expected answer is that certain words that begin with the letter c̲ sound the same at the beginning, as in the words cent and cider.

Invite the children to name other words that have the same beginning sound as cent. Write each word on the board. Ask the children to observe the words and draw another conclusion. They may say, "Certain words that sound the same at the beginning as the word cent begin with the letter c̲" or the letter s̲."

Ask the children to watch for words in their reading that begin with the letter c in order to further check the accuracy of their conclusions.

A teacher should provide opportunities for children to apply the skills.

The authors have not attempted to present an exhaustive set of activities. Rather they have isolated the major components of reading to provide illustrative activities and to suggest materials at the primary and intermediate levels. They hope this book will provide a foundation for teacher-made activities and materials.

RESOURCE MATERIALS

The following resource materials can help teachers locate, plan, and develop reading activities for their classrooms.

Videotapes

1. Four Whole Language videotapes showing Whole Language in use in New Zealand classrooms. Christchurch College of Education, Box 31-065, Christchurch, New Zealand.

2. *Managing Literature-based Classrooms.* National Council of Teachers of English, 1111 Kenyon Road, Urbana, Illinois 61801. First–, third–, and fifth–grade teachers share strategies.

3. *Reading Rainbow / GPN*, P. O. Box 80669, Lincoln, Nebraska 68501. Television adaptations of children's books, "field trip" segments, and reviews of books by children. Primary level.

Filmstrips

Encyclopedia Brown's Information Skills Mysteries. Society for Visual Education, Inc., Dept. TK-8989, 1345 Diversey Parkway, Chicago, Illinois 60614-1299. Four filmstrips.

Computer Software

1. *Chariots, Cougars, and Kings.* Hartley, P. O. Box 431, Dimondale, Michigan 48821. Grades 3–5. Comprehension Skills. (Apple)

2. *Explore-a-Story.* Collamore Educational Publishing, a division of D.C. Heath, William K. Bradford Company, 594 Merritt Road, Lexington, Massachusetts 02173. Grades K–4. (Apple II, 128K)

3. *Kid Writer.* Spinnaker Software, 215 First Street, Cambridge Massachusetts 02142. Grades K–4. (Apple)

4. *Kittens, Kids, and a Frog.* Hartley, P. O. Box 431, Dimondale, Michigan 48821. Grades 1–2. Comprehension Skills. (Apple)

5. *Microzine.* Scholastic Inc., 730 Broadway, New York, New York 10003. Magazine on disk.

6. *The Playroom.* Broderbund Software, Inc., 17 Paul Drive, San Rafael, California 94903-2101. Pre K–2 and special education. (Available for IBM, PC/Tandy, Apple, and Macintosh)

7. *Reading for Meaning with Mother Goose.* Hartley, P. O. Box 431, Dimondale, Michigan 48821. Grades 2–4. Comprehension Skills. (Apple)

8. *Stickybear Reading.* Weekly Reader Software. Optimum Resource, Inc., 10 Station Place, Norfolk, Connecticut 06058. (Apple)

9. *Where in Europe is Carmen Sandiego?, Where in the USA is Carmen Sandiego?* and *Where in the World is Carmen Sandiego?* Broderbund Software, Inc., 17 Paul Drive, San Rafael, California 94903-2101. Grades 5+. Research Skills, Problem-solving Strategies. (Apple)

Magazines

1. *Big Book Magazine.* Scholastic Inc., 2931 East McCarty Street, P . O. Box 7502, Jefferson City, Missouri 65102.

2. *Microzine.* Scholastic Inc., 730 Broadway, New York, NY 10003. Magazine on disk.

3. *Magazines for Children,* edited by Donald R. Stoll. International Reading Association, 800 Barksdale Road, P. O. Box 8139, Newark, Delaware 19714-8139 and Educational Press Association of America, Glassboro State College, Glassboro, New Jersey 08028. Selection aid for choosing children's periodicals.

Materials Related to Literature Use and Reading

1. *Activities for Whole Language and Thematic Teaching,* Creative Teaching Press, P. O. Box 6017, City of Cypress, California 90630. Grade K-1 and Grades 2-3.

2. *The Best of Livewire: Practical Classroom Activities for Elementary and Middle School Students,* edited by Julie M. Jensen. National Council of Teachers of English, 1111 Kenyon Road, Urbana, Illinois 61801.

3. *Caldecott Capers: Activities with 10 Caldecott Medal Winners,* by Roberta Burnett, Jane E. Hahn, and Virginia T. Mealy. Book Lures Inc., P. O. Box 9450, O'Fallon, Missouri 63366.

4. *Celebrate Literature,* by Carol Fox and Margery Sauer. Literature Curriculum Guides for Grades K-6. The Perfection Form Company, 1000 North Second Avenue, Logan Iowa 51546.

5. *Children's Literature in the Reading Program,* edited by Bernice E. Cullinan. International Reading Association, 800 Barksdale Road, P. O. Box 8139, Newark, Delaware 19714-8139.

6. *Class Works!!* A Scholastic Teacher's Resource Club, P. O. Box 11413, Des Moines, Iowa 50380-1413.

7. *A Cluster Approach to Elementary Vocabulary Instruction,* by Robert J. Marzano and Jana S. Marzano. International Reading Association, 800 Barksdale Road, P. O. Box 8139, Newark, Delaware 19714-8139.

8. *Focus Units in Literature: A Handbook for Elementary School Teachers,* by Joy F. Moss. National Council of Teachers of English, 1111 Kenyon Road, Urbana, Illinois 61801. Grades K-6.

9. *Innovations Teaching Guides,* Scholastic Inc., P. O. Box 7502, Jefferson City, Missouri 65102. Guides for using literature selections.

10. *Language Experience Activities,* Second Edition, by Roach Van Allen and Claryce Allen. Houghton Mifflin Company, Boston Massachusetts.

11. *Literature and Young Children,* edited by Bernice E. Cullinan and Carolyn W. Carmichael. National Council of Teachers of English, 1111 Kenyon Road, Urbana, Illinois 61801. Grades K-6.

12. *Literature Mini-Units.* MARI, INC., P. O. Box 92404, Pasadena, California 91109.

13. *Macmillan Literature-Based Reading Activities.* Macmillian, Education Plaza, P. O. Box 938, Hicksville, N. Y. 11802-9820.

14. *The New Read-Aloud Handbook*, by Jim Trelease. Second, Revised Edition. Penguin Books, Viking, Penguin Inc., 40 West 23rd Street, New York, New York 10010.
15. *Perform!* Scholastic Inc., 2931 E. McCarty St., P. O. Box 7502, Jefferson City, Missouri 65102. Readers' theatre, oral language development, creative dramatics. Grades 1–6.
16. *Prereading Activities for Content Area Reading and Learning*, Second Edition, by David W. Moore, John E. Readence, and Robert J. Rickelman. International Reading Association, 800 Barksdale Road, P. O. Box 8139, Newark, Delaware 19714-8139.
17. *Reading Activities in Content Areas*, Second Edition, by Dorothy Piercey. Allyn and Bacon, Boston, Massachusetts.
18. *Reading Aids Through the Grades: A Guide to Materials & 501 Activities for Individualizing Reading Instruction*, Fourth Revised Edition, by David Russell and others. Teachers College Press, New York, New York.
19. *Reading Beyond the Basal Plus,* by Doris Roettger. Perfection Form Company, 1000 North Second Avenue, Logan, Iowa 51546. Teacher's Guides for using children's books to go beyond the basal.
20. *Response Guides for Teaching Children's Books,* by Albert B. Somers and Janet Evans Worthington. National Council of Teachers of English, 1111 Kenyon Road, Urbana, Illinois 61801. Grades K–6.
21. *Semantic Mapping: Classroom Applications,* by Joan E. Heimlich and Susan D. Pittelman. International Reading Association, 800 Barksdale Road, P. O. Box 8139, Newark, Delaware 19714-8139.
22. *Storybook Classrooms: Using Children's Literature in the Learning Center—Primary Grades,* by Karla H. Wendelin and M. Jean Greenlaw. Humanics Ltd., Atlanta, Georgia.
23. *Teaching Reading Skills Through The Newspaper*, Second Edition, by Arnold B. Cheyney. International Reading Association, 800 Barksdale Road, P. O. Box 8139, Newark, Delaware 19714-8139.
24. *Thematic Literature Units for Grades 1-8.* Living Literature, 504 Silver Lane, Sergeant Bluff, Iowa 51054.
25. *A Two-Way Street: Integrating Reading and Writing in the Middle Schools,* edited by Jean E. Brown, Barbara A. Quirk, and Elaine C. Stephens. National Council of Teachers of English, 1111 Kenyon Road, Urbana, Illinois 61801. Grades 6-8.

two

Basic Teacher-Made and Commercial Materials

Some basic materials for the reading program include activity and game books as suggested in Chapter 1, as well as other types of materials, which are discussed in the following sections.

PICTURE FILES

Picture interpretation is a natural step in the process of language development, preceding and accompanying the reading of words. Interpreting pictures helps expand the interpretation skills necessary for comprehension of the abstract ideas encountered in reading.

A rich program of observation and interpretation of pictures should be provided for several reasons:

1. Pictures appeal to pupils.
2. Pictures are fruitful sources of new ideas and experiences.

3. Interpreting pictures aids the development of creative expression.

4. Observing pictures helps develop the ability to recall details, to detect relationships, to note the correct order of events, and to aid in identifying unknown words.

Additionally, picture reading is the basis for map and graph reading. Picture reading can help poor readers in intermediate grades cope with content subjects. In this sense, picture reading is more than just a step toward initial reading instruction.

Several stages or levels of picture reading or interpretation can be noted as children progress:

1. Naming or enumeration (of individual parts)

2. Description (listings of action)

3. Interpretation (of whys and wherefores of action)

4. Narrative interpretation (story of action)

5. Evaluation (judgment of action)

The teacher's file of pictures, usually secured from magazines, discarded books, calendars, book jackets, posters, travel pamphlets, picture maps, and the like, is important instructional material. Questions such as the following can be attached to the back of the pictures:

1. Who are the main characters in the picture?

2. What is the main idea of the picture?

3. What are some details in the picture?

4. What mood is expressed in the picture?

5. What action is anticipated in the picture?

6. What probably occurred just prior to the action in the picture?

Pictures are not, however, complete in themselves. A whole story must be derived from certain suggestive details. It is a real art for children to learn how to interpret all the kinds of pictures they will encounter in life. Observation and interpretation of pictures goes on at different levels. The teacher should attempt to ascertain the student's level of comprehension in picture reading and to help the pupil move from a lower to a higher level. The inexperienced child with little background experience may require relatively simple pictures containing few objects and little irrelevant detail. Advanced pupils can be given pictures that will help them discriminate among shapes, sizes, places, relationships, and arrangement of visual details.

In other picture interpretation activities, children can:

1. Leaf through magazines or illustrated books to find pictures related to a story or topic.
2. Look through books for pictures of various kinds of structures when planning to construct a particular object.
3. Decide upon titles for pictures or ways of classifying and grouping pictures.
4. Use pictures of a child and an adult in disagreement or of two children in disagreement as a basis for talking about handling certain social situations.

Picture reading can also be involved in a unit of work. When working on a topic such as "A Healthy Day," pictures might be included to show sleeping habits, brushing teeth, eating breakfast, putting on outdoor clothes, a school scene, visiting the dentist, preparing an evening meal, and putting objects away.

Other ideas for picture reading include the "What do you think will happen now?" worksheet. In this situation, the teacher puts up one or two pictures that present a precarious situation and invites the children to draw three or four colored pictures that complete the story (see following page.)

At times, children may draw their own sequence pictures after hearing a story. They can then be called upon to arrange the pictured events in the correct order and to retell the story. Or they may draw pictures based on their own personal experiences, such as points of interest in a tour through the school building, or steps in an experiment conducted in the classroom.

There is no easy solution to the problem of picture storage and retrieval. Large pictures, used for bulletin boards, murals, and large displays, will need to be stored in a large flat folder or a map cabinet. Small- and medium-sized pictures (8½ by 11 inches or smaller) can be placed in folders in a filing cabinet. A subject or topic number-accession system is helpful. For example, a file section labeled "Poems" would include pictures related to poems. The individual pictures would be numbered, along with the names of the specific poems. A card file or master list noting the subject picture number, and name of poem would be correlated with the filing system. Similar treatment could be provided for suitable subjects or topics—stories, articles, seasons, holidays, creative expression, specific skills (character study, detail, relationships, and sequence), discussion, self-concept, and content (social studies, science, literature, mathematics). Subtopics might be useful for some major subjects or topic headings. The subjects would be dependent upon the picture collection itself and the purposes for which the files would be used.

FIGURE 2.1

PICTURE SOURCES
   Some valuable materials for use with picture interpretation include
the following:

1. Reading readiness pictures (part of basal series)
2. Filmstrips
3. Golden Book series (Racine, Wis.: Western Publishing Co.)
4. Illustrated trade books (such as *Everybody Needs a Rock*, by Byrd Baylor, New York: Scribner, 1974). (Trade books are those written and marketed through bookstores and libraries for the general public; they are not textbooks.)
5. Flannelboard stories (such as *A Surprise for Mrs. Bunny*, by Charlotte Steiner, New York: Grosset and Dunlap, 1945)
6. Textless (nonverbal) books (*What Whiskers Did*, by Ruth Carroll, New York: H. Z. Walk, 1965)
7. Commercial sets of picture series (such as *Discussion Pictures for Beginning Social Studies*, New York: Harper & Row, 1967 [for grades K–4]; *People in Action Series: Role-playing and Discussion Photographs for Elementary Social Studies*, New York: Holt, Rinehart and Winston, 1970; and *Who Am I?* New York: Sadlier, 1970 [for grades K–1]).

8. Commercial pictures available from such sources as J. L. Hammett Co., Box 4125, Lynchburg, Va. 24502; Giant Photos, Inc., Box 406, Rockford, Ill., 61105; Scholastic Book Services, 50 W. 44th Street, New York, 10036.
9. Content books (science and social studies).

STORY FILES

A file of stories kept on index cards or in a notebook might contain the title, author, publisher, and age level for which the material is most suitable. There should also be a brief summary identifying the plot and the characters. The stories may be categorized as suitable for telling, dramatizing, puppetry, making up other endings, or reading for enjoyment. An example is provided below.

Card: Story File (Primary)

Title: <u>Louie</u>

Publisher: William Morrow, 1975

Ages: 5–8

Illustrated by Keats

Resume: Susie and Roberta plan a puppet show. Louie, who rarely speaks, attends. He is fascinated by the puppet Gussie and starts talking to her. He sits down and gets quiet only when Gussie's voice (Susie) asks him to do so. At the end of the show, Louie is unhappy to see Susie and Roberto take the puppet home. Louie has a sad dream about Gussie, but finds a pleasant surprise when he is awakened.

Suitability/Topics: Read for enjoyment; multi-ethnic; search for a friend.

If the story is to be told, the following sequence of steps are suggested as guidelines for preparing to tell the story:

1. Read the story several times to get the incidents clearly in mind and to get a clear picture of the details.
2. Use a tape recorder to practice telling the story.
3. Use cue cards—opening lines, main points of the story, climax, closing—if they help you.

4. Memorize essential parts that provide atmosphere or imagery, e.g., "In the high and far-off times, O best beloved . . ." or "East of the sun and west of the moon . . ."

5. Retape the story, concentrating upon improvement of pitch, range, and voice. Be sure you are enunciating clearly and that you are making good use of pauses.

6. Use gestures sparingly; do not be overdramatic. Pace the presentation appropriately.

Flannelboard

A flannelboard is a simple and inexpensive piece of material that attracts children's attention and stimulates interest. The following directions indicate how to make one.

Materials:

1 piece of plywood ⅜ × 24 × 32 inches

1 piece of heavy flannel 28 × 36 inches

Cover one side of the plywood with the flannel. Turn excess flannel over edges. Turn under the raw edges, miter corners, and staple.

Some suggestions for use of the flannelboard for storytelling follow:

1. Make flannelboard cutouts of characters and objects in the story.

2. Number each cutout in order of use.

3. After each phase of the story has been told, remove the cutouts and start on the next phase.

4. Vary speed of presentation and volume and pitch of voice.

5. Store cutouts in a labeled box or file for convenient use by the storyteller.

The use of puppets enhances storytelling. Here are some suggestions for making two types of puppets.

Stick Puppets

A stick puppet can be constructed from cardboard by stapling the front and back of the figures together over a long thin stick.

FIGURE 2.2

Hand Puppets

A hand puppet can consist of a head and loose garment. The head can be made of styrofoam or papier-maché. The index finger fits into the neck, and the thumb and middle finger fit into the sleeves.

FIGURE 2.3

STORYTELLING REFERENCES
The following "how-to" references may be helpful to teachers:

Bauer, Caroline F. *Handbook for Storytellers.* Chicago: ALA, 1977.
Ross, Ramon R. *Storyteller.* Columbus: Charles E. Merrill, 1972.
Sawyer, Ruth. *The Way of the Storyteller.* New York: Viking, 1962.

Sawyer, Ruth. "How to Tell a Story". Chicago: F. E. Compton, Division of Encyclopaedia Britannica. 1973.

Wagner, Joseph A. *Children's Literature Through Storytelling.* Dubuque, Iowa: W. C. Brown Co., 1970.

These references contain children's stories for telling:

Arbuthnot, May Hill. *The Arbuthnot Anthology of Children's Literature.* 3rd. ed. Chicago: Scott, Foresman, 1971.

Carlson, Bernice. *Listen: And Help Tell the Story.* Nashville, Tenn.: Abingdon Press, 1965.

Cathon, Laura E. and others. *Stories to Tell to Children.* Pittsburgh: University of Pittsburgh Press, 1974.

Colwell, Eileen. *A Second Storyteller's Choice.* 3rd. ed. N.Y.: H. Z. Walck, 1976.

Johnson, Edna and others. *Anthology of Children's Literature.* 5th. ed. Boston: Houghton-Mifflin, 1977.

Zisland, Sylvia. *Telling Stories to Children.* Chicago: H. W. Wilson, 1976.

POETRY FILES

To be ready with the right poem at the right moment often means having your own poetry collection. Five-by-eight inch index cards or loose-leaf notebooks are convenient for this purpose. Poems may be filed under classifications according to purpose, such as suitability for choral reading, dramatizing, memorizing, or reading for enjoyment. An example is shown below.

Card: Poetry File

Name of Poem: "There Was a Crooked Man," Mother Goose

Ages: 5–7

      Boys: There was a crooked man
      Girls: And he went a crooked mile
      All: He found a crooked sixpence against a crooked stile.
      Boys: He bought a crooked cat,
      Girls: Which caught a crooked mouse
      All: And they all lived together in a little crooked house.

Suitability: Choral speaking (antiphonal)

Type: Humorous

WORD FILES

One idea for a word file is to choose a topic such as "fabrics," list twelve to fifteen words that are related to the topic, and then paste appropriate fabric samples on a piece of oaktag.
An example is given below:

Card: Word File
    Sticky
    Soft
    Fuzzy
    Rough
    Stiff
    Slick

Word charts can be developed with such titles as "Fun Words," "Quiet Words," "Fast Words," "Sleepy Words," or "Words About Sports." Others can be focused on synonyms and antonyms or word families (such as *heart, hearty, heartily, heartless, heartache*). Some can include foreign language words (*sombrero, petite, salon*), while other lists can be developed about occupations (*farmers, mechanics, bankers*) or settings (*hospital, sports arena, library*).

Of value to intermediate level pupils would be word-origin files, such as the one shown below.

Word Card: History of Words (Intermediate)

    Tantalus was a king who for his crimes was condemned to go without water or food. He was made to stand in water that receded when he tried to drink, and with fruit hanging above him that receded when he reached for it. So when we tantalize, we tease or torment by offering something desirable but keeping it out of reach.

    Here are some other words with interesting histories. See if you can write a short story about each one.

boycott	cereal
sandwich	chauvinism
pasteurize	cardigan
gerrymander	raglan
guillotine	spoonerism

Bulletin board displays may be developed from unusual phrases children glean from their reading. Examples of personification, simile, metaphor, euphemism, and hyperbole are excellent to use. A class might compile a list of unusual phrases as shown on the following page.

Unusual Phrases of the Week

    1. She worked like a horse.
    2. The sun smiled down on the workers.
    3. He was a pillar of strength.
    4. Joe has gone to the great beyond.
    5. I've told you that a million times.
    6.
    7.
    8.
    9.
    10.
    11.
    12.

WORD ACTIVITY REFERENCES

Following is a list of trade books that may help in developing word activities.

Asimov, Isaac. *Words from the Myths,* Boston: Houghton-Mifflin, 1961.

Corwin, Judy. *Words, Words, Words, Words,* New York: Platt, 1977.

Feelings, Muriel. *Swahili Counting Book,* New York: Dial, 1973.

Fitzgerald, Cathleen. *Let's Find Out About Words,* New York: Watts, 1971.

Funk, Charles. *Heaven to Betsy,* New York: Warner, 1972.

Funk, Charles. *Horsefeathers and Other Curious Words,* New York: Harper, 1958.

Gwynne, Fred. *Chocolate Moose for Dinner,* New York: Windmill, 1976.

Hanson, Joan. *Sound Words,* New York: Lerner, 1976.

Harmon, Margaret. *Working with Words,* New York: Westminister, 1977.

Janson, Joan. *Homographic Homophones,* New York: Lerner, 1973.
    (Also see, by same author, other titles such as *Homographs, Homonyms, Synonyms, Similes,* and others)

Lindburg, Peter. *What's in the Names of Wild Animals,* New York: Coward, McCann and Geoghegan, 1977.

Nurnberg, Maxwell. *Fun With Words,* Englewood Cliffs, New Jersey: Prentice-Hall, 1970.

Pickles, Colin and M. Laurence. *The Beginning of Words: How English Grew,* New York: G. P. Putnam, 1970.

Provensen, Alice and Martin. *Play on Words,* New York: Random House, 1972.

Rosenbloom, Joseph. *Daffy Dictionary: Funabridged Definitions, from Aardvark to Zuider Zee,* New York: Sterling, 1977.

Schwartz, Alvin. *Tom Foolery: Trickery and Foolery with Words,* Philadelphia: J. B. Lippincott, 1973.

Smith, Elsdon. *The Story of Our Names*, New York: Gale, 1970.
Tremain, R. *Fooling Around with Words*, New York: Greenwillow, 1976.
Wilbur, Richard. *Opposites*, New York: Harcourt, Brace, 1973.
Wolff, Cynthia G. *A Feast of Words*, New York: Oxford, 1977.

FINGERPLAYS, ACTION VERSES, SOUND STORIES, AND MOVEMENT STORIES

The following are are examples of fingerplays, action verses, sound stories, and movement stories.

Fingerplay

From Five to Zero
Here are five fingers, no more, (Hold up hand with fingers spread)
Hide one—and now there are four. (Put down one finger)
Hide another—look, now there are three, (Put down one finger)
Hide another—there are two you see. (Put down one finger)
Hide another—look, now there is only one, (Put down one finger)
Hide it—and there are none. (Hold up clenched fist)

Action Verse

An action poem involves more than the fingers.

Stretching
I lift my hands up high in the air,
And I touch my toes, if I dare.
I place my hands on my hips,
And I touch my feet, making two dips.
I hold my hands on my knees,
And I take five steps forward, if you please.
Then I stand straight, sharp as a tack,
And give a good rest to my back.

Sound Story

Here children supply appropriate sounds as the story is read aloud to them. The dashes represent the places where sounds are to be supplied by the listeners.

One cold day the wind howled — — — and the thunder boomed — — — and the rain pattered — — —. The birds began to chatter — — — and the dogs barked — — — and the horses neighed — — — and the pigs squealed — — —.

Movement Story

Below is a story in which children respond through movement, in the spaces indicated by dashes.

Bill and Betty move their bodies in many ways:
By jumping up and down — — —
By running slowly — — — and fast — — —
By leaping through the air — — —
By taking giant steps — — — and small steps — — —
By bending down — — —
By reaching up — — —

REFERENCES
For some excellent sources of fingerplays, action verses, sound stories, and movement stories, see:

Burroughs, Margaret T. *Did You Feed My Cow?* Chicago: Follett, 1969.
Carlson, Bernice. *Listen! and Help Tell the Story.* Nashville, Tenn.: Abingdon Press, 1965.
Grayson, Marion. *Let's Do Fingerplays.* New York: Luce, 1965.
Matterson, Elizabeth. *Games for the Very Young, A Treasury of Nursery Songs and Finger Plays.* New York: American Heritage Press, 1969.
Scott, Louise B. and J. J. Thompson. *Rhymes for Fingers and Flannelboard.* New York: McGraw-Hill, 1960.
Wagner, Guy, et al. *Games and Activities for Early Childhood Education.* Darien, Conn.: Teachers Publishing Corp., 1967.
Yamaguchi, Marianne. *Fingerplays.* New York: Holt, Rinehart and Winston, 1970.

ACTIVITY FILES

Reading activities often seem less like assignments if made available to children on individual cards, filed according to category. Such cards are often referred to as "activity cards" or "task cards." See sample below.

Literature Activity Card   (Primary/Intermediate)

Go the literature center. Select a tape, record, filmstrip, videotape, or film for listening or viewing. You may choose someone to share this with you. When you have finished, fill out a slip and put it in your folder.

Name _____

Name of story _____

Author _____

(Check one) Tape ____ Record ____ Filmstrip ____ Other ____

I saw/listened alone   Yes ____   No ____

I shared this with _____

I (we) enjoyed this   Yes ____   No ____

Other comments:

SPECIAL WORKSHEETS

Some materials will need to be structured to help differentiate instruction; for example, special worksheets should be provided for the linguistically gifted and for the slower learner, as well as for the average learner. A sample worksheet is shown below.

Worksheet: Language in Literature (Intermediate)

A. Do the following:
1. Go to the listening center.
2. Read "The Tale of Custard the Dragon" by Ogden Nash.
3. Listen carefully to the record of "Custard the Dragon".

B. Answer these questions and do these exercises.
1. Describe Belinda's friends (other than Custard) who lived with her in the little white house.
2. Describe the appearance of Custard.
3. What words were used over and over to describe Belinda's pet dragon?
4. Draw a picture of what you think the pirate looked like.
5. What is meant by "grog in the pocket flagon"?
6. Write a further adventure for Custard. If possible, use Nash's verse form; prose form is also satisfactory.

INSTRUCTIONAL BULLETIN BOARD DISPLAYS

Often a bulletin board display can be used to present an idea, such as shown below.

Challenge of the Day

These words and definitions appear in Samuel Johnson's Dictionary of the English Language, 1755. Try to write pairs of sentences using each word to show its meaning 200 years ago and its meaning today.

Whitewash — A wash to make the skin seem fair

Tremendous — Dreadful; horrible

Toot — To pry; to peep

Overnight — Night before bedtime

Catsup — A kind of pickle, made from mushrooms

Penthouse — A shed hanging out aslope from the main wall

Sherbet — The juice of a lemon or orange mixed with water and sugar

Uncouth — Odd; strange; unusual

INSTRUCTIONAL CHARTS

Charts on various reading topics may be prepared and posted as reminders. These may be developed by the teacher, or, more probably, cooperatively by the teacher and children. The following is an example.

Decoding Unfamiliar Words

Step 1. Apply context clues.

Step 2. Try the sound of the initial consonant, vowel, or blend along with context clues.

Step 3: Check for structure clues (prefixes, suffixes, inflectional endings) with context clues.

Step 4: Begin sounding out the word, using known phonic generalizations. (Go only as far as necessary to determine pronunciation of the word.)

Step 5: Consult the dictionary.

CONTRACT CARDS

Some teachers find that they are able to provide highly individual assignments and tasks by negotiating them with individual pupils. The agreement can even be formalized through the use of a contract signed by teacher and pupil. The contract simply states what the pupil is to do and when the task is to be completed. Once agreed to, the contract should be completed as specified by the deadline.

A teacher can prepare and have available contracts calling for a variety of assignments and tasks from which pupils can select those that most suit their needs, or the pupils themselves can propose contracts and negotiate them with the teacher. The contract can, of course, take many forms. One form is shown below.

A Sample Pupil Contract Format   (Primary)

1. In magazines find pictures of 4 things that begin with the same sound as "dog" and "doll".
2. Draw pictures of 4 things that begin with the same sound as "dog" and "doll".
3. Write 4 words that begin with the same sound as "dog" and "doll".
4. Find 4 things in the room that begin with the same sound as "dog" and "doll". Put a tag on them.

I will do _____ and _____ for my contract.

My name _____ Today's date _____

Teacher's name _____ Date due _____

A modification of the contract plan is sometimes called an assignment or job sheet. In making such a sheet, the teacher first identifies a definite instructional goal—for example, the mastery of a specific skill or some subskill—and then organizes available material (textbook/workbook, etc.) so that the learner is guided toward that goal. Each child can proceed as fast as mastery permits. At times children can work in twos or threes to complete the assignment, which may take from three to five class periods. Below is shown a sample.

Job Sheet: Finding details (name of book)

Page	Directions
7	You and your partner take turns in reading paragraphs together. Then read, answer, and check questions 1 and 2.
15	You and your partner take turns in reading paragraphs together. Then do work as directed on the lower half of page 15.
33	Read, answer, and check questions on lower half of page 33.
42	Do sections 2 and 5 as directed.
67	Read and discuss this section with your partner; answer questions at bottom of page 67.
72	Working alone write, as directed; when finished, check your work with your partner.
80	Complete the blanks in the bottom right corner of page 80. Check your answers in the Teachers' Edition.

Go to teacher for a review discussion and a check test, before picking up your next assignment sheet.

STUDY GUIDE SHEETS

Because children's reading should be purposeful, students could use study guides when reading content materials. These guides are duplicated sheets prepared by the teacher and distributed to children to help guide reading in content fields and alleviate difficulties that interfere with understanding. Study guides can provide purposes for reading as well as aids for interpretation of the material. A selection and a sample study guide follow.

Study Guide Sheet

Hazards Along The Way

Crossing the plains was dangerous, but at least the wagons rolled along at a fairly steady pace. Crossing rivers, mountains, and deserts was another matter.

Where a shallow river had to be crossed, the wagons were usually driven through. Often the mules or oxen became unruly as they felt the water swirling around them. It took all the efforts of experienced drivers to get the animals to pull together and cross the stream. Some of the men had to walk alongside the wagons, lifting wheels out of the sand or mud and helping to keep the wagons from overturning and spilling their cargoes into the water.

Sometimes the water was too deep for the wagons to cross. Then one wagon was usually sealed to make it waterproof so that it could be used as a ferry or raft to float all the cargoes across. That meant unloading and reloading each of the wagons for each river crossing.

Going through the mountains, the wagons had to be hauled up steep slopes on one side. Then, on the downhill side, they had to be weighted with dragging trees to keep them from rolling out of control. When the caravan started out, each family carried all their belongings, including family treasures and furniture, in the covered wagons. But as they crossed one barrier after another, they often had to leave precious keepsakes behind to lighten the load. It was not at all unusual to see a large, highly polished chest of drawers or even a piano at the edge of a river or in the middle of a desert.

The Oregon Trail was not for the weak or the easily discouraged. There was the weather—often too hot or too cold, too dry, too wet, or too windy. There were days when wagons broke down and had to be repaired. There were accidents and spells of sickness, with no doctors or medicines for a thousand miles or more. There were places where a wrong turn might lead a hundred miles out of the way. There were days of thirst with no fresh water in sight, and days of hunger when the food they carried with them ran out and they could find no fish or game on the trail. There were Indians and herds of stampeding buffalo. But however difficult the journey, thousands of men, women, and children survived the hardships to reach Oregon in safety.

Source: Lands of Promise by Merle Prunty and E. B. Fincher, N. Y.: Macmillan Co., 1971, pp. 223-24.

---

1. Read the first three paragraphs to find out the dangers of crossing rivers.
   What is the meaning of unruly? Swirling? Experienced? Cargoes? Waterproof?
   Describe how they crossed if the water was very deep.
2. Read the fourth paragraph to discover how they crossed the mountains.
   What is meant by these words: Slopes? Weighted? Barrier? Keepsakes? Chest of drawers?
   How did the caravans go through the mountains?
3. Read the last paragraph to find out other dangers of traveling on the Oregon Trail.
   What is the meaning of the word game in this paragraph?

Notice that the last paragraph described five or six other hardships endured by the travelers. What were they? What are spells of sickness?
4. Write one sentence to summarize what the writer was trying to say about the people who travelled along the Oregon Trail.
5. Look back at the map of the Oregon Trail on page 222. Imagine you are a member of a wagon train. Be prepared to describe your feelings.

SKILL FILES

Skill files may be nothing more than pages cut from various grade level workbooks, which are then grouped according to skill and filed by levels in a file cabinet or box. Reading skills lend themselves particularly well to this type of organization.

When a student needs additional practice with a particular reading skill, one or more worksheets at the correct level of difficulty can help.

Commercial and teacher-made worksheets can be reused if they are mounted on oaktag and covered with clear contact paper or laminated with a drymount press so that pupils can write on them with grease pencils or water-soluble markers. Each sheet should be labeled or color-coded with the following information: level of difficulty, skill, and worksheet number. They can be made self-checking either by pasting answers on the back or by having the answers in a separate file nearby. If multiple copies of each worksheet are prepared, several pupils can work on one activity simultaneously.

Teachers can find learning materials other than worksheets to include in a file of this nature. Games, transparencies, filmstrips, and audiotapes can be prescribed for individual or small-group use without direct teacher supervision.

LEARNING CENTERS

Many of the activities presented in this book can be modified easily to be part of a learning center.

Basically the features of a learning center activity include (a) an objective, (b) materials, (c) task cards, and (d) evaluation. Often a pre- and post-test are administered in conjunction with the activity. An example involving homonyms follows.

Objective: Children will be provided practice in recognizing homonyms.

Pre- and Post-Test: Put "T" for True and "F" for False beside each statement.

    ____ 1. "Cooked" and "raw" are pronounced alike.
    ____ 2. "Write" and "right" are homonyms.
    ____ 3. "Wide" and "broad" are *not* homonyms.
    ____ 4. "Hear" and "here" sound the same.
    ____ 5. "Sad" and "happy" are homonyms.

Materials Needed:

A packet (containing prepared cards naming homonyms) and a game board, as illustrated on the following page.

Task Card:

Choose a partner. Play "Concentration" as explained on the "Concentration Direction Card".

Concentration Direction Card

On the board are 30 cards, numbered from 1 to 30. Under each of these cards is a homonym. There are 15 homonym pairs. The object of the game is to match the homonyms with each other. This is how to play the game: Player A picks a number, for example, Number 1, which has the word "road" under it. Player A tries to choose a homonym for "road". He or she chooses Number 19 which has the word "rode" under it. Player B checks the answer list and finds that the words match. Then Player A scores a point, and he or she continues to pick until he or she fails to obtain a match. After Player A looses his or her turn, Player B then goes through the same process as Player A did. The game continues until the board is cleared of cards, and the player with the most points wins. (Note: When a match is made, the cards which were matched are removed from the board.)

Variation:

Synonyms and antonyms also can be used in the game with adaptations. Sample lists follow.

Synonyms	*Antonyms*
big/large	slow/fast
hurried/rushed	big/small
ask/inquire	weak/strong
almost/nearly	fat/skinny
error/mistake	ugly/pretty
fast/quick	old/young
frightened/scared	
sad/unhappy	

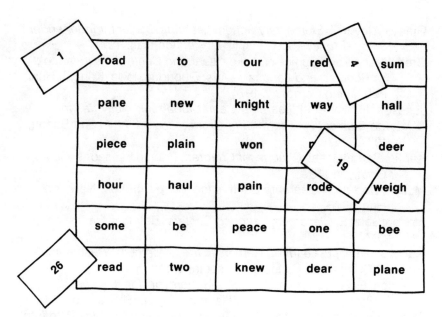

	road	to	our	red	9	sum
	pane	new	knight	way		hall
	piece	plain	won			deer
	hour	haul	pain	rode		weigh
	some	be	peace	one		bee
26	read	two	knew	dear		plane

FIGURE 2-4
Evaluation: Self-checking.

REFERENCES FOR LEARNING CENTER
Following is a list of materials about learning centers:

Bennie, Frances. *Learning Centers: Development and Operation.* Englewood Cliffs, N.J.: Educational Technology Publications, Inc., 1977.

Blake, Howard E. *Creating a Learning-Centered Classroom.* New York: Hart, 1976.

Crabtree, June. *Learning Center Ideas.* Cincinnati, Ohio: Standard Publisher, 1977.

Davidson, Tom. *Learning Center Book.* Salt Lake City, Utah: Goodyear, 1976.

Dick, Norma. *Ideas for Reading Learning Centers.* Sacramento Calif.: California Reading Association, 1973.

Fisk, Lori. *Learning Centers.* Glen Ridge, N.J.: Exceptional Press, 1974.

Forte, Imogene and Joy MacKenzie. *Nooks, Crannies, and Corners.* Nashville, Tenn.: Incentive Publications, Inc., 1972.

Forte, Imogene, et al. *Center Stuff for Nooks, Crannies, and Corners.* Nashville, Tenn.: Incentive Publications, Inc., 1972.

Horton, Lowell. *The Learning Center: Heart of the School.* Minneapolis, Minn.: Denison, 1973.

Glasser, Joyce F. *Elementary School Learning Center for Independent Study.* Englewood Cliffs, N.J.: Prentice-Hall, 1971.

Greff, Kasper, and Eunice N. Askov. *Learning Centers: An Ideabook for Reading and Language Arts.* Dubuque, Iowa: Kendall/Hunt Publishing Company, 1974.

Johnson, Hiram, et al. *Learning Center Ideabook: Activities for the Elementary and Middle Grade.* Boston: Allyn and Bacon, 1977.

Kaplin, Sandra, et al. *Change for Children.* Pacific Palisades, Calif.: Goodyear, 1973.

Maxim, George W. *Learning Centers for Young Children.* New York: Hart, 1976.

Morlan, John E. *Classroom Learning Centers.* Belmont, Calif.: Fearon, 1974.

Nations, Jimmy E. *Learning Centers in the Classroom.* Washington, D.C.: National Education Association, 1975.

Peterson, Gary T. *Learning Center: A Sphere for Non-Traditional Approaches to Education.* Hamden, Conn.: Shoestring, 1975.

Ptreshene, Susan S. *A Complete Guide to Learning Centers.* Palo Alto, Calif.: Pendragon House, 1977.

Rapport, Virginia. *Learning Centers: Children on Their Own.* Washington, D.C.: Association for Childhood Education International, 1970.

Thomas, John I. *Learning Centers: Opening Up the Classroom.* Boston: Holbrook Press, 1975.

Waynant, Louise and Robert M. Wilson. *Learning Centers: A Guide for Effective Use.* Paoli, Penn.: McGraw-Hill, 1974.

INDEPENDENT STUDY PLANS

An example of an independent study plan is provided below. (Such a plan is also referred to as a Learning Activity Packet or a LAP.)

How To Use This Individualized Study Plan

1. Take pre-test.
2. If this test suggests there is much to be learned about using the Dewey Decimal System of Classification, proceed with this plan.
3. Study the Introduction.
4. Study the Behavioral Objective for Lesson 1, then do one or more of the activities suggested.

5. Take a self-test for Lesson 1. Use Lesson 1 self-test key on page 37 to check answers. If some of the answers are incorrect, use the card catalogue and the books on the shelves to find the right answers.

6. Proceed through lessons 2 and 3 the same way.

7. Take post-test.

DEWEY DECIMAL SYSTEM OF CLASSIFICATION PRE-TEST
Draw a line under the right answers.

1. The Dewey Decimal System of Classification has (5) (10) (20) main classes.

2. Each class groups books according to (subject) (color) (size).

3. Books that are in the same class are put on the shelf (anywhere) (together) (apart).

4. The call number of a book contains a (number) (letter) (number and letter).

5. The letter in a call number stands for the first letter of the author's (last name) (first name) (middle name).

Using the Dewey Decimal System of Classification as a guide, write the class name and number (in hundreds) for the following books.

	Class Name	Class Number
1. *What Is a Bird?*	_____	_____
2. *Days We Celebrate*	_____	_____
3. *Famous Paintings*	_____	_____
4. *About Truck Farming*	_____	_____
5. *The Christ Child*	_____	_____

Write the call number for the following books. Use the card catalogue.

1. *Science Can be Fun* by Munro Leaf   _____

2. *America is Born: A History for Peter* by Gerald W. Johnson   _____

3. *Abraham Lincoln* by Clara Ingram Judson   _____

4. *Games* by Jessie Bancroft   _____

5. *Mind Your Manners* by Betty Allen   _____

The Dewey Decimal System of Classification

INTRODUCTION

Have you ever gone into a large supermarket to buy something? Did you wander up one aisle and down the other looking for the item? If you continued looking, you probably noticed that the counters were numbered, and that there were signs telling the names of the products in each aisle. These numbers and names told you where to go to find certain products.

Have you ever gone into a library to find a certain book that you were eager to read? Sometimes it is hard to find one small book among several thousand unless you know where to look. The library also has numbers and signs (class names) to help you. These numbers and signs are called the Dewey Decimal System of classification.

This Individualized Study Plan is designed to help you become acquainted with the Dewey classes (signs) and numbers, but more important, it will help you use the system as a tool for finding books in this library, other school libraries, and public libraries.

The first lesson tells the story of the Dewey Decimal System of Classification and why the author grouped certain books into one class so they would be put on the shelf together.

Pretend you are starting on a treasure hunt. Let the Dewey Decimal System of Classification give you clues to finding good books to read this year. It can be a very exciting adventure.

MAJOR IDEA:

The Dewey Decimal System is an important tool in learning to use the library.

COMPONENT IDEAS:

1. The Dewey Decimal System of Classification is a system devised by Melvil Dewey that is used in many libraries.
2. Books are grouped together according to subject matter.
   a. Each group has a certain number.
   b. Books with the same number are shelved together.
3. The Dewey Decimal System of Classification is a helpful guide to finding books in the library.

BEHAVIORAL OBJECTIVES (There is one lesson for each objective.):

1. Given ten books, the learner will tell which broad (hundreds) Dewey classification they should be placed in with 90 percent accuracy.
2. Given a list of ten titles, the learner will write these titles in their proper classification with 80 percent accuracy.
3. Given a list of ten books the learner will write the Call Numbers with 80 percent accuracy.

Lesson 1
How the Dewey Decimal System of Classification Was Started

Some years ago Melvil Dewey devised a system of classifying books that is used today in many libraries. He chose certain main subjects and numbers, so that all nonfiction books on the same subject would be together on the shelf. He chose these subjects by imagining himself to be a primitive person. He asked himself questions he thought such a person would have asked. These are the groups he chose and the numbers he assigned to them:

100—Philosophy and Psychology
200—Religion
300—Social Sciences
400—Philology (Language)
500—Science
600—Applied Science and Useful Arts
700—Fine Arts and Recreation
800—Literature
900—History, Geography, Biography
000—General Works (Bibliographies, encyclopedias, and other reference books)

ACTIVITIES (Choose one or more of these activities.)
1. Take a tour of a library. Using the Dewey Decimal System of Classification as a guide, find books in different subject areas.
2. Choose a nonfiction book that you are interested in reading. Look at the call number and decide what subject area it is in.
3. View a filmstrip on the Dewey Decimal System of Classification.

TEST I
Write the correct class number after each of the following titles:
1. *The French ABC* _____
2. *The Christ Child* _____
3. *All About Dinosaurs* _____
4. *Know Your Government* _____
5. *The American Revolution* _____
6. *Engines* _____
7. *Their Search For God* _____
8. *Time for Poetry* _____
9. *Famous Paintings* _____
10. *How We Get Our Cloth* _____

Reread the story of the Dewey Decimal System and then fill in the blanks with words or numbers.

1. Melvil Dewey divided all knowledge into _____ main classes.
2. All nonfiction books with the same _____ are together on the library shelf.
3. All books about religion are numbered _____ .
4. Man communicates with others by use of _____ .
5. Books that help man enjoy his leisure time are classed as _____ and

_____ .

Lesson 2
Organizing Nonfiction

Carpenters need tools to build houses. Plumbers need tools to put in pipes. Painters need tools to paint houses. You need tools to find books in the library. In the first lesson you learned about the Dewey Decimal System of Classification. This is a tool to help you find books on different subjects on the library shelves. Now you are ready to use this knowledge to organize nonfiction books into the correct classes.

ACTIVITIES (Choose two or more of these activities.)
1. Look at ten book jackets of nonfiction books. Write or tell someone the class name and number for each book. Check the shelf or card catalog to see if you are right.
2. Read one nonfiction book on any subject and give a short informal book report on it. Ask the class if anyone knows the class name and number.
3. Play a Dewey Decimal game called "What class is it?" this way: Have a stack of index cards with titles on one side and class names and numbers on the other. Hold up a title and see if your partner can give the class and number. If he answers correctly, he gets the card; if he makes a mistake, you keep the card.

TEST II
Write the titles in their proper classifications in the spaces that follow.
1. *Daniel Boone* by Esther Averill
2. *Manners Can Be Fun* by Munro Leaf
3. *Owls* by Herbert Zim
4. *Favorite Poems Old and New* by Helen Ferris
5. *You Can Write Chinese* by Kurt Weis
6. *Golden Encyclopedia* by Dorothy Bennett
7. *Real Book About Baseball* by Lynn Hopkins
8. *Book About God* by Florence Fitch

9. *How Your Body Works* by Leo Schneider
10. *The Story of the Civil War* by Red Reeder

000–099 General Works

_____

100–199 Philosophy (None)

200–299 Religion

_____

300–399 Social Sciences

_____

400–499 Language

_____

500–599 Science

_____

600–699 Applied Science and Useful Arts

_____

700–799 Fine Arts and Recreation

_____

800–899 Literature

_____

900–999 History, Geography, Biography (two titles)

_____

_____

Lesson 3
Dewey Decimal Classes Subdivided

In Lessons 1 and 2 you have learned how important it is to be able to use the ten main classes in the Dewey Decimal System of Classification to find books in the library.

To make it still easier to find books on the shelves, each of the ten main classes is further divided into nine subdivisions. Example:

500 Science	540 Chemistry	580 Botany
510 Mathematics	550 Earth Science	590 Zoology
520 Astronomy	560 Prehistoric Life	
530 Physics	570 Biology	

ACTIVITIES (Choose two or more.)
  1. Use flash cards with authors and titles on one side and call numbers on the other. Working with a partner, see how many call numbers you can correctly name.
  2. Go to the card catalogue and find the call numbers for at least five books in five different classes. Find these books on the shelves.
  3. Make a list of three subjects you are interested in. Find one or more books on each subject and list the call numbers.

TEST III
Write the call number for each of the following titles.*
  1. *Manners to Grow On* by Tina Lee ____
  2. *The 26 Letters* by Oscar Ogg ____
  3. *The First Book of Painting* by Moore Lamont ____
  4. *The Costume Book* by Joseph Leeming ____
  5. *Poems* by Rachel Field ____
  6. *Looking at Ancient History* by R. J. Unsted ____
  7. *The First Book of Music* by Gertrude Norman ____
  8. *New Plays and Red Letter Days* by Janette Woolsey ____
  9. *Fossils* by Frank Rhodes ____
  10. *All About the Human Body* by Bernard Glemsel ____

Quest Activities:

  1. Keep a record of several of the books you check out this year. Indicate if they are nonfiction, fiction, or easy by writing the call number, F, or E after the titles.
  2. If you have a hobby, choose two or three books that tell about it. Share with the class in one or more of these ways:
     a. Bring something you made and describe how you made it.
     b. Bring some kind of collection, such as a rock collection or insect collection, and tell about it.
     c. Tell some interesting experience, such as cooking a meal for the family or going fishing.
     d. Draw a picture to illustrate your hobby.
     e. Give an oral book report on one of the books you have chosen and show the class some of the illustrations in it.

---

* You may use the Dewey class numbers with special subdivisions in *Library Skills: Using the Dewey Decimal System,* Book II, by Margaret V. Beck and Vera Pace, p. 21.

f. Share with the class a magazine article dealing with your hobby which was referred to in one of the books.

3. Keep a portfolio of illustrations of books on different subjects. Indicate the call number and classification of each book.

4. Make up a Dewey Decimal game to help others learn to find books on different subjects.

Teacher–Pupil Conferences

1. When you need help please feel free to talk it over with the teacher.
2. When you have decided on any of the activities in Lessons 1-3, or the quest activities, tell the teacher.
3. When you have finished an activity, tell the teacher.
4. If you have any suggestions as to how the teacher can make the Dewey Decimal System of Classification any easier to understand, please tell her or him.

Answer Key

KEY TO PRE-TEST

1. 10
2. subject
3. together
4. number and letter
5. last name

CLASS NAME
1. Science
2. Social Science
3. Fine Arts
4. Applied Science
5. Religion

CALL NUMBER
1. 500
   L
2. 973
   J
3. 921
   L

CALL NUMBER
(continued)
4. 790
   B
5. 395
   A

CLASS NUMBER
500
300
700
600
200

KEY TO TEST I
1. 400
2. 200
3. 500
4. 300
5. 900
6. 600

KEY TO TEST I
(continued)
7. 200
8. 800
9. 700
10. 600

1. 10
2. subject
   (or number)
3. 200
4. Language
5. Fine Arts
   and Recreation.

KEY TO TEST II		KEY TO TEST III	
000–099	General Works	1.	395
	Golden Encylopedia		L
100–199	Philosophy	2.	411
200–299	Religion		O
	Book about God	3.	750
300–399	Social Sciences		M
	Manners Can Be Fun	4.	391
400–499	Languages		L
	You Can Write Chinese	5.	811
500–599	Science		F
	Owls	6.	930
600–699	Applied Science and Useful Arts		U
	How Your Body Works	7.	780
700–799	Fine Arts and Recreation		N
	Real Book About Baseball	8.	812
800–899	Literature		W
	Favorite Poems Old and New	9.	560
900–999	History, Geography, Biography		R
	Daniel Boone	10.	612
	The Story of the Civil War		G

LISTENING CENTERS AND OTHER RESOURCES

A listening center is usually a specific place in the classroom. It has to be near electric outlets. Audiovisual equipment and materials are the main materials required; particularly desirable are a record player and records, a tape recorder and tapes, and a filmstrip projector and filmstrips. Filmstrips without words printed on them are also interesting to work with. Using a recorder, childern can compose their own commentaries to go with the filmstrips and then share them with others.

Recordings of stories are available from the following sources:

1. Caedmon Records, 505 Eighth Avenue, New York (records, tapes, and cassettes of children's stories).

2. Miller-Brody Productions, 342 Madison Avenue, New York ("talking books").

3. Scholastic Audio-Visual Materials, Englewood Cliffs, N.J. (record—book companion series).

4. Spoken Arts, Inc., 310 North Shadeland Avenue, New Rochelle, N.Y. (many materials on cassettes: fairy tales, fables, poems, stories and tales from other lands).

5. Weston Woods, Weston, Conn. (records and cassettes of children's stories).

Teachers in many states are required to take an introductory course in educational media. Even if not required, such a course usually is helpful in aiding teachers to better prepare and use teacher-made and commercial materials, particularly of the kinds discussed in this chapter.

three

Prereading Experiences

In 1959 David Ausubel characterized readiness as the relation between the adequacy of existing capacity and a given learning task's demands. Readiness is a factor at all reading levels, though it is most frequently associated with beginning or first-grade reading, that is, the gradual development from nonreading to beginning reading.

A question frequently asked is: Should formal reading instruction begin in the nursery or kindergarten years? The authors feel that any time a child is eager for help in this area, he or she should be encouraged. The idea of introducing reading to children who meet the criteria of readiness has merit, but there are many other important functions of the early school years. In brief, all young children should be challenged and aided to grow toward reading, but need not necessarily be offered a formal program of reading instruction before first grade.

PREREADING FACTORS

There are a number of prereading factors: experiential background, general language facility, concepts of reading, visual discrimination, and auditory discrimination.

Experiential Background

This factor is an important consideration in developing the concepts and vocabulary needed to interpret the printed word. When a child sees the word *horse,* he or she should associate it with a mental image of a horse. This abstraction is impossible unless a child has formed some mental images of the concepts being presented. Three major procedures are used to develop experiential background. First is sensory experience. A young child is eager to engage in activities designed to involve the five senses—sight, sound, touch, taste, and smell—as a means of perceiving his or her surroundings. In doing so, he enlarges his speaking and listening vocabulary. Second, through listening to stories and poems read by the teacher, the child is provided with a good model of voice use, pacing, word choice, and pronunciation. Third, through the use of learning centers, many opportunities can be provided for the development of eye-hand coordination, listening skills, and speaking skills such as sharing, conversing, comparing, and explaining, as well as visual discrimination and vocabulary development.

General Language Facility

Speaking ability and listening comprehension are important factors in prereading. Young children learn the techniques of conversing from other children and from adults. Both spontaneous and organized conversations help children to express their own ideas, think about the ideas of others, and plan and evaluate critically. Sharing is another avenue for oral expression, whether a child is describing something made or done during class or sharing an out-of-school experience. Storytelling is yet another valuable oral expression experience. Children can analyze and interpret illustrations in books and use dramatic play and puppetry as techniques of presenting literature. Children explain, direct, compare, and evaluate as they participate in learning centers of various types, particularly the drama or role-playing ones. Study units or projects evolving around a central theme also provide an abundance of real and vicarious experiences that furnish ideas and facts to talk about. And, of course, class trips and resource persons provide still more opportunities for oral expression.

Similarly, many opportunities for listening exist in daily activities. For example, children learn to follow directions by participating in various forms of drama (such as finger plays and sound stories). Answering questions based upon a story read by the teacher is another way to develop the thinking process, oral language skills, and listening skills. Children can retell familiar stories in sequential order, detect irrelevant sentences inserted in a paragraph read by the teacher, listen to descriptions provided by the teacher, and take turns telling what they think the teacher has described.

The listening center also can provide further opportunities for development of vocabulary and listening comprehension.

These types of activities are preparation for reading, since before learning to read, children must have adequate speaking and listening vocabularies that will help them understand printed words and sentence structure. If a child comes across the word *cat* and is able to sound it out but does not have the word *cat* as a part of his speaking or listening vocabulary, it will not make any sense to him. When he looks at the word cat, he should associate it with a mental image of a cat. Meaning is impossible to discern unless the child has formed some mental images of the words and concepts presented in the reading selection.

Concepts of Reading

Listening to stories and poems read aloud is one of the finer ways to promote an interest in learning to read. In interpreting illustrations in books, children can be led to discover significant characters, main ideas, details, mood, and probable future action. Gradually, finer discriminations may be made regarding shape, size, place relations, and visual details. At an early age, children begin to tell and interpret stories and poems on their own. Storytelling is one literary activity that does not depend upon reading ability; thus, through this medium every child can improve speech patterns, poise in speaking, and ability to organize events in proper sequence. Experience charts and stories may be done individually or cooperatively by a group of five or six children. Dictation of experience charts and stories effectively establishes the important language relationships—that is, the relationship of an experience (with its ideas, structure, and inherent significance) to its manifestation first in oral language, then in written form, and finally in reading what has been written. A library center within the classroom is a significant component in developing concepts of reading, oral comprehension, and oral expression. Through its use, children can learn that books have a front and back, that the words in them are arranged from the top to bottom and from left to right, and that the pages are numbered in a particular sequence.

Visual Discrimination

This skill enables children to see similarities and differences in letters and words. Before a child can read, he or she must be able to see the difference between *d* and *b, day* and *bay,* and so forth. This skill is also needed for writing. Discrimination between lower and upper-case letters must be taught since in many instances their shapes differ. Teaching the concepts of *same* and *different* is in fact one of the first tasks in working with visual discrimination.

Auditory Discrimination

Not only must children see the similarities and differences among letters, they must learn the different letter sounds, to distinguish, for example, between *m* and *n; man* and *can.* Simple poems and jingles can be used to draw attention to rhyming words. At times saying a word that does not begin with same sound as three other words in a group provides an excellent contrast in letter-sound discrimination. Children must hear differences in sounds before they can begin to associate symbols with sounds. The names of the letters must be taught because letters are usually referred to by name when the sound/symbol relationships are introduced. For example, when teaching children to associate *t* with /t/, it is convenient to refer to the sound by its letter name.

Based upon the preceding discussion of major reading factors, specific types of informal checklists may be prepared to help the teacher in the assessment of a child's reading readiness.

Chart 3.1.   Checklist for Reading Readiness (Yes—No)

A. Concept and Vocabulary
Does the child:
_____ seem to possess mental images of common concepts?
_____ know common terms of position (up and down, etc.), sequence
          (first and last, etc.), size (small and large, etc.), and the like?
_____ know names of common objects or things?
B. Language Facility
Does the child:
_____ listen attentively and with understanding?
_____ follow oral directions?
_____ express experiences clearly?
_____ tell connected stories?
_____ follow and tell ideas in sequence?
C. Reading Concepts
Does the child:
_____ possess left-to-right orientation?
_____ interpret pictures?
_____ prepare picture-story sequences?
_____ recognize letter sequence in words?
D. Motor and Visual Discrimination
Does the child:
_____ possess good eye-hand coordination?
_____ copy forms of varying shapes?
_____ discriminate and recognize letters and words?
_____ know the names of the printed alphabet letters?

E. Auditory Discrimination
Does the child:
_____recognize rhyming words?
_____discriminate differences in sounds associated with letters?
_____associate consonant and vowel sounds with letters?

COMMERCIAL PREREADING MATERIALS AND REFERENCE SOURCES

In the phase of instruction labeled by educators as prereading or emergent literacy, a wide variety of materials should be used to promote language learning. The references below include both materials to be used with children and reference sources for teachers of young children.

COMPUTER SOFTWARE

1. *Curious George in Outer Space*. DLM Teaching Resources, P. O. Box 4000, One DLM Park, Allen, Texas 75002. Concept Development for *tall* and *short, long* and *tall, big* and *small*. (Apple II, 64K)
2. *Stickybear ABC*. Weekly Reader Software. Optimum Resource, Inc., 10 Station Place, Norfolk, Connecticut 06058. (Apple)
3. *Stickybear Opposites*. Weekly Reader Software. Optimum Resource, Inc., 10 Station Place, Norfolk, Connecticut 06058. (Apple)

APPROPRIATE MAGAZINES FOR THE PREREADING LEVEL

The following magazines are useful at the prereading level. For more information about most of these magazines and others, consult Magazines for Children, Donald R. Stoll, Editor. Copyright 1990 by the International Reading Association, Inc., 800 Barksdale Road, P. O. Box 8139, Newark, Delaware 19714-8139, and Educational Press Association of America, Glassboro State College, Glassboro, New Jersey 08028.

1. *Big Book Magazine*. Scholastic Inc., 2931 East McCarty Street, P. O. Box 7502, Jefferson City, Missouri 65102.
2. *Highlights for Children*. P. O. Box 269 Columbus, Ohio 43272-0002. General interest magazine. Ages 2-12.
3. *Let's Find Out*. Scholastic, 2931 East McCarty Street, P. O. Box 3710, Jefferson City, Missouri 65102-9957. Themed issues. Pre K-K.
4. *Letterbug*. 111 Hillcrest Avenue, Beaver Falls, Pennsylvania 15010. Language and literature focus. Ages 3-6.
5. *Sesame Street Magazine*. P. O. Box 52000, Boulder, Colorado 80321-2000. Preschool activities. Ages 2-6.
6. *Your Big Backyard*. National Wildlife Federation, 8925 Leesburg Pike, Vienna, Virginia 22180. Conservation. Ages 3-5.

OTHER PRIMARY GRADE PREREADING AND READING RESOURCES

1. *Cooking Up a Story* and *Super Story Telling,* by Carol B. Catron and Barbara C. Parks. T. S. Denison & Company, 9601 Newton Avenue South, Minneapolis, Minnesota 55431. Pre K-Grade 2.
2. *EUREKA Treasure Chest.* A Whole Language Shared Reading Program from Australia. McDougall, Littell, P. O. Box 1667, Evanston, Illinois 60204. Pre K-Grade 7.
3. *Fun with Action Stories,* by Joan Daniels. T. S. Denison & Company, 9601 Newton Avenue South, Minneapolis, Minnesota 55431. Pre K-Grade 2.
4. *Learning to Love Literature: Preschool Through Grade 3,* edited by Linda Leonard Lamme. National Council of Teachers of English, 1111 Kenyon Road, Urbana, Illinois 61801.
5. *Storytelling with the Flannel Board: Book 1,* by Paul Anderson and Irene Francis; Book 2, by Paul Anderson; and Book 3 by Idala Vonk. T. S. Denison & Company, 9601 Newton Avenue South, Minneapolis, Minnesota 55431. Pre K-Grade 2.

BOOKLETS AND BROCHURES FOR PARENTS

The following booklets and brochures are all available from the International Reading Association, 800 Barksdale Road, P. O. Box 8139, Newark, Delaware 19714-8139.

BOOKLETS

1. *Beginning Literacy and Your Child,* by Steven B. Silvern and Linda R. Silvern. 1990. (Copublished with ERIC/RCS).
2. *Creating Readers and Writers,* by Susan Mandel Glazer. 1990.
3. *You Can Help Your Young Child with Writing,* by Marcia Baghban. 1989.
4. *Helping Your Child Become a Reader,* by Nancy L. Roser. 1989. (Copublished with ERIC/RCS)

BROCHURES

1. *Good Books Make Reading Fun for Your Child,* by Glenna Davis Sloan.
2. *You Can Encourage Your Child to Read.*

The remainder of this chapter consists of games and activities designed to promote and reinforce emergent literacy.

CONCEPT AND VOCABULARY DEVELOPMENT

3.1   Match Concept Game

Objective: To provide practice with classifying and categorizing
Materials:
 Large sheet of oaktag, with captions
 16 picture cards to fit squares, as illustrated:

FIGURE 3-1

Directions: Divide the oaktag into 2-inch squares, as shown in
illustration. At the top of the section, print concept words and affix a
sample picture of each word. Appropriate words are *animals* (bear,
cat, dog, horse), *fruit* (apple, orange, banana, pear), *people* (boy, girl,
woman, man), and *toys* (toy airplane, wagon, truck, scooter).
 The child arranges the picture cards under the appropriate
concepts.

Variation:

Some other concepts and accompanying words follow.

House	Clothes	Colors	Shapes	Food	Numbers
door	shirt	red	circle	cheese	1
window	pants	blue	triangle	hot dogs	2
stairs	socks	black	square	beans	3
roof	tie	brown	rectangle	corn	4
chimney	coat	white	sphere	soup	5

Name the Objects   3.2

Objective: To extend the child's vocabulary through labeling objects in a picture

Materials:

Set of pictures, as follows:
Picture of a small boy. He is putting food in the bowl for his cat. The cat scratches and bites the boy. The boy yells and spills the food on the cat.

Directions: Ask the child to find and describe the objects and actions in the pictures, such as *blue jeans, sweat shirt, cat food, cat collar, kneeling child, cat scratches boy, boy's surprise.*

Variations:

1. Use the objects and actions to launch other discussions. For example, *child* can be used to discuss parts of the body, such as arm, ankle, feet, fingers, legs, ears, head, neck, waist. A *kitchen scene* can launch discussion about a stove, table, dish, cup, or bowl; a *bedroom* could lead to talk about a bed, lamp, desk, closet, and pictures; a *living room,* about a television, chair, rug, and couch; and a *garage,* about a car ladder, gas cans, tools, etc.
2. The following picture books are all useful in eliciting good discussions.

PICTURE BOOKS

Alexander, Martha. *Bobo's Dream.* New York: Dial Press, 1974.
Ardizzine, Edward. *The Wrong Side of the Bed.* New York: Doubleday, 1970.
Carle, Eric. *Do You Want to Be My Friend?* New York: Crowell, 1971.
_____. *I See a Song.* New York: Crowell, 1973.
Carroll, Ruth. *The Christmas Kitten.* New York: Walck, 1970.
_____. *The Dolphin and the Mermaid.* New York: Walck, 1974.

Goodall, John S. *Ballooney Adventures of Paddy Pork.* New York: Harcourt Brace Jovanovich, 1969.
Goodall, John S. *Paddy's Evening Out.* New York: Atheneum, 1973.
Goodall, John S. *Naughty Nancy.* New York: Atheneum, 1975.
Hutchins, Pat. *Changes, Changes.* New York: Macmillan, 1971.
Kent, Jack. *The Egg Book.* New York: Macmillan, 1975.
Krahn, Fernando. *Who's Seen the Scissors?* New York: Dutton, 1975.
Lisker, Sonia. *Lost.* New York: Harcourt Brace Jovanovich, 1975.
Mayer, Mercer. *Bubble Bubble.* New York: Parents Magazine Press, 1973.
Mayer, Mercer. *Frog Goes to Dinner.* New York: Dial, 1974.

3.3 Relate the Words

Objective: To extend the child's acquaintance with relationship words

Materials:
Picture, as illustrated

Directions: The child identifies each object in the picture as the words are spoken by the teacher.

FIGURE 3.3

Variations:
1. Many excellent trade books can be used to develop concepts and vocabulary. The concepts are noted in parentheses.

Aliki. *My Five Senses.* New York: Crowell, 1962. (ourselves)

Busch, Phyllis S. *City Lots.* Cleveland, Ohio: World, 1970. (environment)

Crews, Donald. *We Read: A to Z.* New York: Harper, 1969. (words)

Emberly, Ed. *The Wing on a Flea: A Book about Shapes.* Boston: Little Brown, 1961. (shapes)

Hoban, Tana. *Count and See.* New York: Macmillan, 1972. (numbers)

Krasilovsky, Phyllis. *The Very Little Boy.* New York: Doubleday, 1962. (size)

Lobel, Arnold. *The Great Blueness and Other Predicaments.* New York: Harper, 1968. (color)

MacDonald, Golden. *Red Light, Green Light.* New York: Doubleday, 1944. (opposites)

Schick, Eleanor. *City in the Winter.* New York: Macmillan, 1970. (seasons)

Spier, Peter. *Crash! Bang! Boom!* New York: Doubleday, 1972. (sound)

Young, Miriam. *If I Drove a Train.* New York: Lothrop, 1972. (transportation)

2. Play a game using prepositions. Example: put an object *in* (*on, under, beside, below, above, behind*) a box and ask children to identify the various positions.
3. Play a game with adverbs. Example: have students show walking *quickly, slowly, sadly, quietly, noisily, happily*, etc.
4. Play a game with adjectives. Example: ask students to pretend they are *big, little, brave, happy, unhappy, kind, old, young*, etc.
5. Play a game with verbs. Example: have students demonstrate *walking, running, hopping, working, playing.*

LANGUAGE FACILITY

Feel and Tell 3.4

Objective: To provide children opportunities for oral expression and vocabulary development

50 Chapter 3

Materials:
> Miscellaneous objects, such as a soft eraser, a pencil, a cotton ball, sandpaper, a key, a checker, a small plastic bottle, a soft-drink cap, a cork, and a spool of thread.

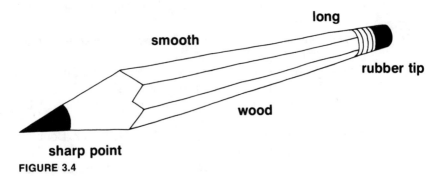

long
smooth
rubber tip
wood
sharp point
FIGURE 3.4

Directions: Gather five or six sacks full of miscellaneous, unrelated objects. Divide children into teams of five or six. One child in each group is the leader, and he selects an object from a sack, but keeps it hidden from the rest of the group. Without naming it, he describes what he feels in his hand, and the other children try to guess what the object is. The child who guesses correctly receives one point and becomes the leader.

Variation: Divide the players into two teams. A player from each side receives an object, and in turn, gives clues to his teammates, who try to guess the object. The teacher times each team, noting how long it takes each to answer correctly. The team with the least amount of accumulated time wins the game.

3.5 Do As I Say

Objective: To provide practice in listening carefully to directions

Materials:
> Sheet of blank paper
> Crayons

Directions: Say to the class, "Listen carefully and do exactly what I say." Then give several simple directions, such as:
> Draw a red line near the top of your page.

Draw a black cat near the middle of your page.
Take a yellow crayon. Write the first letter of your name near the
bottom of the page.
Variation: Play the game on other occasions, giving increasingly
complex directions, such as "Draw a ball," "Put a blue-mark (x) on the
ball," or "Draw a line from the cat to the dog."

READING CONCEPTS

Reproducing the Sequence 3.6

Objective: To impress upon children that words have a particular
sequence of letters
Materials:
Envelopes
3 × 5 inch cards
Directions: Print the children's names on separate envelopes. Print
the letters of each child's name on an index card and cut out the
separate letters. Put these letters in the envelope with the child's
name on it. Tell each child to select the envelope with his or her name
on it and take out the letters and arrange them in their proper
sequence.

MOTOR AND VISUAL DISCRIMINATION

Copy the Forms 3.7

Objective: To help children further develop eye-hand coordination
and the ability to recognize gross differences
Materials:
A copy of the worksheet that follows for each child

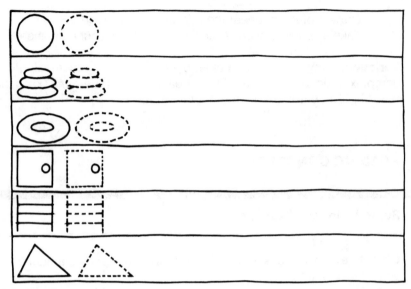

FIGURE 3.7

Directions: Ask pupils to complete each dotted figure and then try to make another one just like it.

3.8 Match the Letters and Words

Objective: To provide practice in visually discriminating letters and words

Materials:
Worksheets, as follow, for each child
Crayons

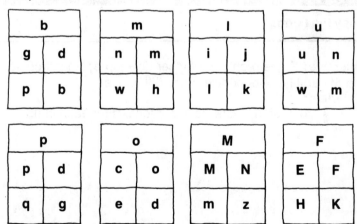

FIGURE 3.8

then	
them	than
that	then

bad	
dad	bat
bad	bed

went	
went	want
when	what

pat	
bat	mat
pet	pat

man	
can	ran
man	pan

can	
can	cab
cat	cad

Directions: Ask children to color in the blocks that contain the same letter or word as the one above the figure.

The Letter Name Game 3.9

Objective: To provide practice in recognizing and saying letter names
Materials:
  Spinner
  Markers
  Game board, illustrated as follows:

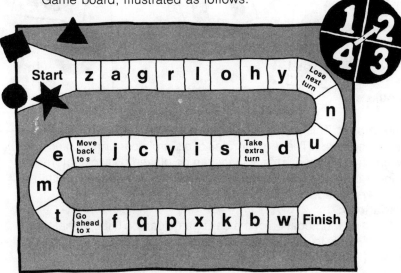

FIGURE 3.9

Directions: Each player uses the spinner to determine how many spaces to move. He or she says the letter name on the space where the marker lands. The game ends when one player has gone from Start to Finish three times.

3.10   Letter Card Game

Objective: To provide practice in associating upper and lower case letters

Materials:

Set of 52 cards, 26 with lower case letters and 26 with upper case letters, illustrated as follows:

FIGURE 3.10

Directions: This game is one in which a child accumulates pairs of matching cards. The regular rules of a simple card game, such as Old Maid, may be used. This activity can be played by two or more. The winner is the one who matches the most cards correctly within a specified period.

Variations:

1. A modification of the card game can be used in matching only lower case letters (make two sets of lower case letter cards).

2. A similar modification of the card game can be used in matching upper case letters (make two sets of upper case letter cards).
3. Another activity is matching words with words.
4. Only the more difficult letters and words may be utilized in the card game (as b/d; u/n; p/g; m/w; n/m; p/d; p/b; o/c; and then/them; bad/dad; went/want/ pat/bat) after letters and words of gross differences have been utilized (as g/t; man/boat).
5. Phrase-matching cards may be utilized as suggested in this activity.

AUDITORY DISCRIMINATION

Rhyming Picture Game 3.11

Objective: To provide practice with rhyming words
Materials:
Sets of picture cards, cut from magazines and pasted on cards
Box large enough to hold cards

FIGURE 3.11

Directions: There should be about 24 picture cards—about 10 sets that rhyme and 4 other words that do not. A sample set might consist of such words, as

boat, coat	man, pan	apple
cat, rat	bug, rug	duck
fish, dish	jar, star	egg
house, mouse	fan, can	kite
rake, cake		

The child is to match the rhyming cards. Code the backs of the pictures with a color or other symbol so the child can self-check. For example, the cards *hat* and *bat* could have a red dot on the back.
Variation: Two or more children compete against each other. Shuffle the cards and place face down. Place three cards face up on the table. Each child draws a card in turn. If he can rhyme his card with one of the face-up cards, he keeps both cards. If not, he adds his card to the face-up ones. The game continues until all rhyming cards have been claimed. The child who has the most cards is the winner.

3.12 Hang the Cards

Objective: To provide children with practice in associating beginning sounds of words with letters
Materials:
    Cothesline
    Clothespins labelled with letters
    Picture cards of common objects
Directions: Attach a series of the labelled clothespins to the clothesline. The children choose appropriate picture cards for the letter sounds and attach them to the appropriate clothespin. Samples follow.
    p—pig, pencil, pail, pin, pear
    t—turtle, table, tree, turkey, tape
    h—house, horse, hand, hammer, hair
    b—ball, bottle, bed, boat, bear
    s—sun, stick, star, soap, sand
Variations:
    1. Print a letter (such as "p") on a container covered with
       attractive paper. The children choose appropriate picture
       cards for the letter and place these cards in the container

Two or three containers with different letters and two or three sets of picture cards may be used at the same time.

2. Construct a "b" truck. Using picture cards, ask the children to fill the truck with pictures beginning with the sound represented by that letter.

3. This activity can be adapted to ending sounds or medial sounds.

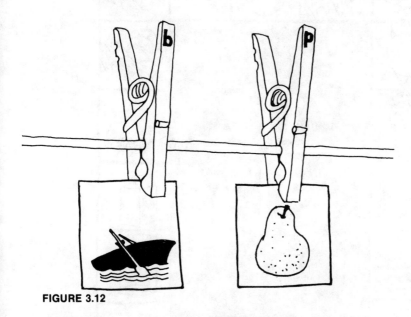

FIGURE 3.12

Around the Block With the Same Sound 3.13

Objective: To provide practice with auditory discrimination (initial sounds)

Materials:
Game board, illustrated on following page
Spinner
Markers

Directions: Two or three players may participate. Each player places his or her marker at Start. The players take turns spinning the spinner to see how many spaces to move. When moving, the player must say a word that begins with the same sound as the picture beneath his or her marker or return to his or her original space. The game ends when one player has gone around the block three times.

Variation: The game can also be played as a five-game series, with the winner being the first person to win five individual games.

FIGURE 3.13

four

Word Recognition

The goal of reading instruction is to help children become independent readers. If this goal is to be achieved, students must learn a number of methods of word recognition, and they must learn to be flexible in the use of these methods, applying the particular word-recognition techniques that fit each situation they encounter. They must realize that sometimes more than one technique will be needed to help them decode an unfamiliar word.

Word-recognition skills include the development of a sight vocabulary and a number of word-attack skills, such as use of context clues, phonics, structural analysis, and dictionary use to aid in word identification. Teaching a single word-recognition method is unwise because certain techniques work better in particular situations than do others. Additionally, some students learn certain word-recognition techniques more readily than they learn others, and teaching a single approach places a handicap on a child who has great difficulty with that particular approach. For example, a child with an auditory handicap may experience difficulty in applying phonics generalizations for decoding purposes, but may do well with context clues.

Sight words are words that are recognized immediately without any need for analysis. One goal of a good reading program is to turn the words that a reader encounters repeatedly in his or her reading material into sight words. Having a large store of sight words makes reading more fluent and rapid. This generally enhances comprehension because the child's train of thought is not continually interrupted in order to analyze unfamiliar words. Then, too, many irregularly spelled words in the English language fail to lend themselves to phonic analysis and are best learned as sight words. In addition, a store of regularly spelled sight words can be the basis for an analytic phonics approach.

Context clues are used by examining the words and sentences surrounding an unfamiliar word in order to determine what word makes sense in relationship to the context. If pupils have a word in their oral vocabularies, but have not encountered it in printed form, context clues can help them produce the word that fits into the sentence logically. Context clues that reveal the meaning of the unfamiliar word are called semantic clues. Another type of context clue is called a syntactic clue. Children can use syntactic clues because they have been speaking English for several years, and they have a feeling for the syntax of the language. Therefore, they can often tell from syntactic clues whether an unfamiliar word is a noun, verb, adjective, or some other part of speech. For greatest accuracy, context clues should be used in conjunction with other word-recognition skills. Using phonic or structural-analysis skills to check a word determined through use of context clues discourages wild guessing.

The term *phonics* refers to associating speech sounds (phonemes) with printed symbols that represent the sounds (graphemes). In English this sound-symbol association is not absolutely regular, but there is sufficient regularity to make possible the decoding of a large percentage of the words that children encounter in their reading material if appropriate phonic generalizations have been taught. Mastery of phonic skills is an important stage in becoming an independent reader. Because phonic analysis does not always result in the correct pronunciation of a word (e.g., as with irregularly spelled words) and because it is considerably slower than some other word-recognition methods, it should be used in conjunction with other techniques.

Structural-analysis skills involve identification of prefixes, suffixes, and root words; inflectional endings; contractions; compound words; and syllabication and accent. When decoding words through structural analysis, units larger than the single graphemes considered in phonic analysis are used. Prefixes and suffixes are affixes (groups of letters) added to root words to form new words called derivatives. The result is a change of meaning and/or a change in the part of speech of the root word. Prefixes are placed before root words, and suffixes are placed after root words (*un* in unrelated; *ful* in joyful). Inflectional endings are groups of letters that, when added to nouns, change the number (*s* in girls), case (*'s* in girl's), or gender (*ess* in hostess); when added to verbs, change the tense (*ed* in waited) or person (*s* in walks); and when added to adjectives change the degree (*est* in meanest). They also may change the part of speech of a word (*ly* in slowly). The new words that are produced by adding inflectional endings are called variants. Contractions are words that consist of combinations of two words with one or more letters omitted. The missing letters are indicated by an apostrophe (can't for cannot). Compound words are composed of two words that, when combined, form a new word (cowboy). Since many phonics generalizations apply not only to single syllable words, but also to syllables within multisyllabic words, syllabication and accent are important structural-analysis skills.

When other word-recognition techniques fail to produce results, the final approach is use of a dictionary. This approach should be considered a last resort because it is the slowest method and it interrupts the stream of reading. Comprehension may suffer if there are too many delays to look up words.

In order to use a dictionary to decode an unfamiliar word, the reader must be able to use the pronunciation key of the dictionary, along with basic consonant sounds, to interpret the phonetic spellings. He or she also will need to be able to interpret accent marks used in the spellings.

The remainder of this chapter consists of games and activities that can be used to teach and reinforce word-recognition skills.

SIGHT WORDS

Sight Word Football (Primary/Intermediate) 4.1

Objective: To provide practice in recognizing sight words
Materials:
  Chalkboard and chalk *or*
  A sheet of unlined paper or poster board
  Felt-tip marker
  Small football-shaped cutout
  Index cards with sight words written on them
Directions: Redraw the illustration on the chalkboard, the unlined paper, or the poster board. Place the football cutout at the fifty yard line, as shown in the drawing. Place the word cards in a face down stack.

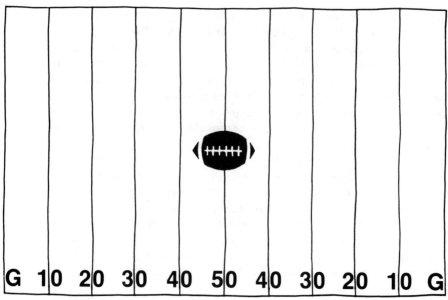

FIGURE 4.1

The game can be played by two students or two teams. The players turn the word cards up one by one. The first player pronounces the word on the first card. If the word is correctly pronounced, the football is advanced ten yards toward the goal, and the child or someone on his or her team draws the next card. This procedure continues until a word is missed or until the ball reaches the goal line. If a word is missed, the other child or team has a chance to pronounce the words and move the ball in the opposite direction. When the ball reaches the goal line, the child or team in control scores six points. This child or team is then allowed to name another word to make the extra point. After the extra point is made or missed, the ball is returned to the fifty-yard line and the opposing team takes its turn.

4.2   Climb the Ladder (Primary/Intermediate, depending on words used)

Objective: To provide practice in recognizing sight words
Materials:
      Piece of poster board
      Stick-on picture hooks
      Color cards with holes punched in them, one for each player
      Scissors
      Index cards with sight words written on them

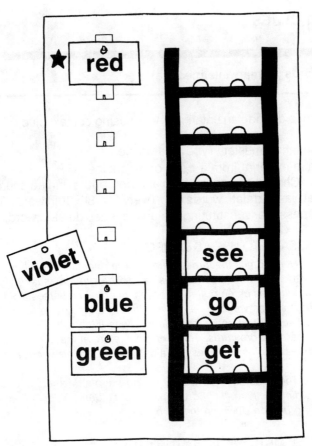

FIGURE 4.2

Directions: Draw a ladder on the piece of poster board. Cut out tabs on each rung of the ladder so that the sight word cards can be inserted. (This allows the words to be changed periodically.) Attach a picture hook beside each rung of the ladder.

Give each child an opportunity to climb the ladder by reading each of the sight words, beginning at the bottom rung and moving toward the top. If a child misses a word, he hangs his color card beside the last rung that he read correctly and listens as other children climb the ladder. Children who climb all the way to the top hang their color cards by the star. After every child has had a turn, the ones who missed words earlier are allowed to start where their color cards are hanging and try to finish the climb to the top.

CONTEXT CLUES

4.3   Missing Words (Primary/Intermediate)

Objective: To decode an unfamiliar word using context clues
Materials:
   Duplicating master, Typewriter or pen
   Textual material from a book or magazine
Directions: Choose a passage from an appropriate printed source.
On a regular basis, delete words (i.e., every 5th, 8th, 10th word). Type
or write the passage, substituting a blank for each deleted word.

SAMPLE PASSAGE TO USE AS SOURCE:

> *Here comes the circus parade! The ringmaster is sitting in the
> front wagon, holding a whip in his hand. The strongman is driving the
> wagon, which is being pulled by a team of prancing horses. Following
> the ringmaster's wagon is a clown with big feet, a white face, and a
> big red nose. Next come the animal cages filled with lions, tigers,
> and other wild creatures. Three elephants are at the end of the
> parade—two full-sized ones and a baby. What fun this circus is going
> to be!*
>
> *The street is lined with cheering people. Mothers and fathers
> are holding their small children on their shoulders. Older children are
> jumping up and down on the curb.*

SAMPLE MATERIAL FOR STUDENTS;

Here comes the circus _____! The ringmaster is
sitting _____ the front wagon, holding _____
whip in his hand. _____ strongman is driving the
_____, which is being pulled _____ a team of
prancing _____. Following the ringmaster's wagon
_____ a clown with big _____, a white face, and
_____ big red nose. Next _____ the animal cages
filled _____ lions, tigers, and other _____
creatures. Three elephants are _____ the end of the
parade—_____ full-sized ones and a _____.
What fun this circus _____ going to be!
   The _____ is lined with cheering _____.
Mothers and fathers are _____ their small children on
_____ shoulders. Older children are _____ up
and down on _____ curb.

Distribute copies of the typed material to the students.
Ask them to read the passage and fill in the blanks with the correct

words. When they have finished, discuss the appropriateness of the words they have chosen. Ask the children to identify context clues that helped them decide which words were appropriate. Accept all meaningful responses.

Severed Sayings (Intermediate) 4.4

Objective: To decode an unfamiliar word using context clues
Materials:
   Duplicating master, Typewriter or pen
Directions: Compile a list of familiar sayings. Type them on duplicating masters, deleting a key word in each (e.g., A _____ in time saves nine). A sample worksheet follows.

Severed Sayings
Directions: Fill in the blanks with the missing words.
   1. A _____ in time saves nine.
   2. Early to bed, early to rise, makes a man healthy, wealthy and _____.
   3. A bird in the hand is worth two in the _____.
   4. Better _____ than sorry.
   5. Better late than _____.
   6. Look before you _____.
   7. If the _____ fits, wear it.
   8. Don't count your _____ before they're hatched.
   9. Don't put all your _____ in one basket.
   10. An apple a day keeps the _____ away.

   Distribute the worksheets to the pupils. Ask them to complete each saying by supplying the correct word. Make an answer key available so that the children can check their own answers.

PHONICS

Initial Sounds Race (Primary) 4.5

Objective: To provide practice in recognizing initial sounds (consonants, vowels, consonant blends, consonant digraphs) in words

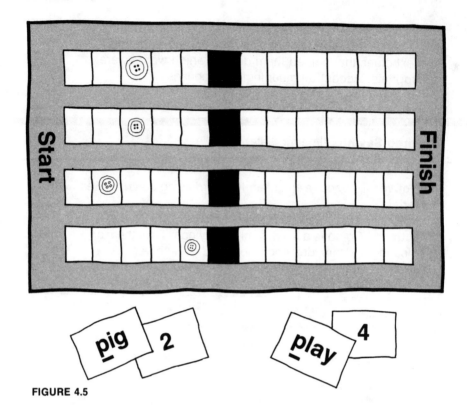

FIGURE 4.5

Materials:
>An old game board or piece of cardboard covered with unlined paper, illustrated above
>Felt-tip pen
>Markers for players
>Index cards with words on one side and numbers from 1 to 4 on the other

Directions: Let each player choose a marker and place it on the starting block of his or her lane. The cards are shuffled and placed on the table with the word on the top card showing. The first player must name another word that has the same initial sound as the one on the top card. If he misses, he does not move; if he is correct, he turns the card over and moves the number of spaces indicated on the back of the card. If the first player misses, the second player must use the same card. If the first player is correct, the second player removes the top card from the stack and responds to the word on the second card. After a player has crossed the darkened sixth space, he must move back one space each time he misses. The first player to cross the finish line wins.

***

Find the Rhymes (Primary) **4.6**

Objective: To provide practice in recognizing rhyming words
Materials:
Construction paper or poster board
Pen or felt-tip marker
Scissors
Directions: Cut egg shapes out of the construction paper or poster board. Cut a zigzag line through each egg to "crack" it. Put rhyming words on the egg halves.

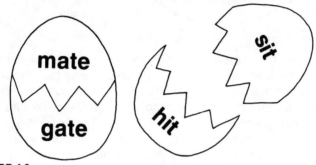

FIGURE 4.6

Mix up the egg pieces and let the children match the egg halves that contain rhyming words. After the halves have been combined, the children can be asked to read the rhymes they have produced and name another word that would rhyme with each pair.

***

Word Wheels (Primary) **4.7**

Objective: To provide practice in blending initial sounds with word endings
Materials:
Poster board
Compass
Scissors
Paper fasteners
Felt-tip pen

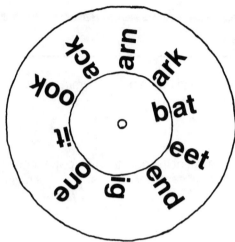

FIGURE 4.7

Directions: Use the compass to draw two circles on the poster board. Make one approximately two inches larger in diameter than the other one. Join the two disks at their centers with a paper fastener. Write a consonant, consonant blend, or consonant digraph on the small disk. Write phonograms on the large disk. Place the consonant, consonant blend, or consonant digraph near the edge of the inner circle and the phonograms near to the center circle, so there is no break between the two parts of the words. (Some children cannot blend a word if they cannot see the word as a whole.)

Ask the child to rotate the outer circle, pronouncing each word that is formed on the wheel by blending the beginning sound with the word ending.

4.8   Magic *E* (Primary)

Objective: To provide practice in recognizing the influence a silent *e* has on some words.

Materials:
>   Strips of poster board (8½″ × 4″ and 6″ × 4″)
>   Metal rings
>   Felt-tip pen

Directions: Cut several 6″ × 4″ strips of poster board, and then one 8½″ × 4″ strip. Write words whose vowel sounds can be changed by a final *e* on the short strips. Write an *e* on the right side of the longer

FIGURE 4.8

strip. Punch two holes in the tops of the strips and insert metal rings, as shown in the illustration.

Have the pupils flip through the shorter strips, pronouncing first the word written on the shorter strip and then the word formed by the addition of the final e. The pupils may be instructed to place their right hands over the e on the base card when pronouncing the shorter word.

Sample words:

rat	rate	cut	cute
bit	bite	tap	tape
hat	hate	hop	hope
kit	kite	fin	fine
mat	mate	can	cane
rot	rote	rip	ripe
strip	stripe	pin	pine

Postman (Primary) 4.9

Objective: To provide practice with long vowel sounds and short vowel sounds

Materials:

Eleven small boxes

Index cards with vowel labels written on them, as shown in illustration

Tape

Pictures of objects whose names contain a single vowel sound

FIGURE 4.9

Directions: Cut slits in the tops of boxes. Tape an index card to each box, and label the last box "other," as shown in illustration.

Give a pupil the pictures and tell him or her to "mail" the pictures in the correct boxes. If the vowel sound in a picture's name is neither long nor short, the child should mail the picture in the *other* box.

4.10   C Worms (Primary)

Objective: To provide practice with the hard and soft *c* sounds
Materials:
    Colorful paper
    Pen
Directions: Draw two worm heads and several worm segments for each worm head. Place an *H* on one worm's forehead and an *S* on the other worm's forehead. Write words containing hard and soft *c* sounds on the worm segments, as shown in the illustration.

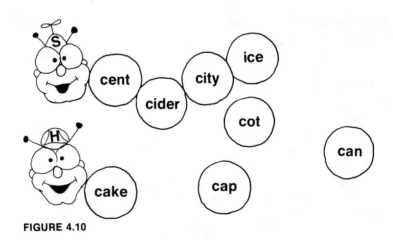

FIGURE 4.10

Let one child take the *H* head and another child take the *S* head. Place the remaining segments in a stack, face down. Let each child draw a segment in turn. If it has the sound for his worm (hard for *H* and soft for *S*), he adds it to his worm. If it has the wrong sound, he must return the segment to the bottom of the stack. He must pronounce the word to claim it. If he tries to claim a word incorrectly, his opponent gets to use it. The first child to complete a worm is the winner.

Variation: Use hard and soft sounds of the letter *g*. Use words such as *gem, gymnasium, gun, game, gone,* and *good.*

STRUCTURAL ANALYSIS

Automobile Affixes (Intermediate) 4.11

Objective: To provide practice with common prefixes and suffixes
Materials:
    Poster board
    Pen
    Scissors
Directions: As shown in the illustration, draw the outline of a car on a sheet of poster board. Cut out several door forms and wheel forms. Write root words on the door cutouts and prefixes and suffixes on the wheel cutouts. Leave one wheel cutout blank.

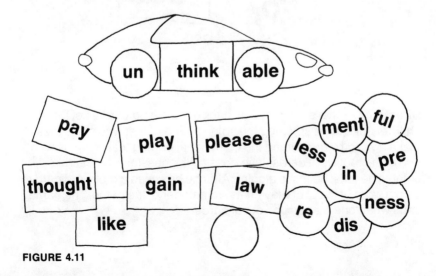

FIGURE 4.11

Let two children or teams take turns making words with affixes by using the wheel and door cutouts. Each child or team gets one point for a word made with a root word and either a prefix or a suffix and two points for a word made with a root word and both a prefix and a suffix. If a child makes a non-word, he loses a point.

4.12 Spin an Ending (Primary/Intermediate)

Objective: To offer practice with common inflectional endings
Materials:
> Spinner with inflectional endings written around the edge
> Index cards with root words written on them

FIGURE 4.12

Directions: Give each player a stack of root word cards. Let the children take turns spinning the spinner. The player who spins tries to make a word by combining the inflectional ending that he spins with one of his root word cards. If he does so successfully, he earns a point. If he fails, he loses a point. After he has used a root word card to form a word, it is out of play for the remainder of the game. The game ends when one player runs out of cards.

Contraction Lace-Up (Primary/Intermediate)   **4.13**

Objective: To provide practice in recognizing words from which contractions have been formed

Materials:

    Poster board

    Yarn or string cut in short strips

    Paper fasteners

    Felt-tip marker

Directions: On one side of the poster board list common contractions in a column. On the other side list the words from which the contractions were formed. Punch holes beside the entries on each side. Place paper fasteners in the holes. Attach pieces of yarn or string strips to the fasteners beside the contractions.

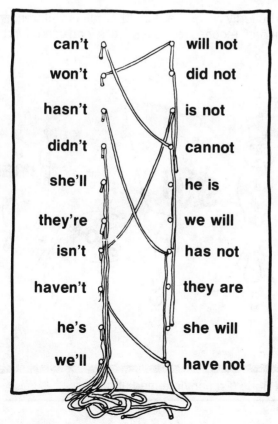

FIGURE 4.13

The child attaches the free end of the yarn or string to the fastener beside the words from which each contraction has been formed. An answer card showing the correct lacing can be made available to the child.

4.14 **Compound Word Match-Up** (Primary/Intermediate)

Objective: To provide practice with compound words
Materials:
>   Poster board
>   Scissors
>   Felt-tip pen

Directions: Cut out butterfly shapes from the poster board. Write parts of compound words on the wings. Cut the butterflies into two pieces.

Mix up the butterfly wings. Let a child, a pair of children, or a small group of children reconstruct butterflies to form compound words.

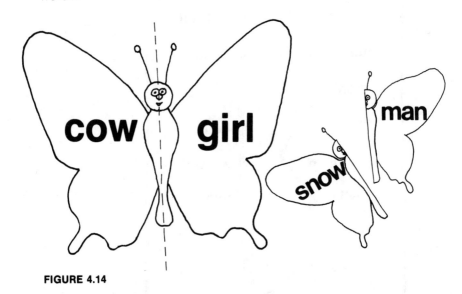

FIGURE 4.14

4.15 **Syllable Search Race** (Primary/Intermediate)

Objective: To provide practice in recognizing the number of syllables in words

Materials:
> Gameboard-sized piece of poster board
> Felt-tip marker
> Spinner labelled with numbers 1 to 4 .
> Sheet of paper
> Tokens for players (buttons or other similar materials)

Directions: As shown in the illustration, draw the race route on the poster board. Write words with different numbers of syllables in the spaces. Make a key for the game on a sheet of paper.

Players place their game tokens on the START space. One person acts as a monitor and does not play. Each player, in turn, spins the spinner. If he spins a 1, he must move his token forward to the nearest one-syllable word on the board. The monitor checks to make sure that the word is actually a one-syllable word. If the player is correct, he leaves his token on the word. If he is incorrect, he must return to start. If the player spins a 2, he must move to a two-syllable word, and so on. On each turn the child must move to the next appropriate word that is ahead of his position on the board. The first player to reach the END wins. END counts as the final one-syllable word in the game. Therefore, to win, a player must spin a 1.

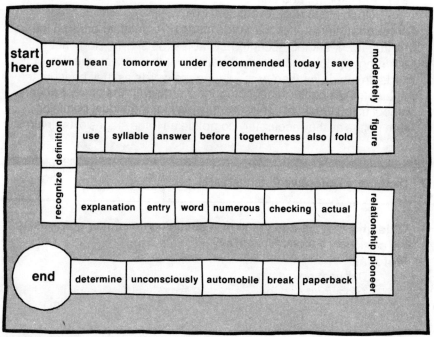

FIGURE 4.15

Variations:
1. Intermediate grades: Require the player to divide a word into syllables when he or she lands on it.
2. Primary grades: Place pictures instead of words on the squares, and let the players move to the picture whose name has a certain number of syllables in it. Auditory skills are involved in this variation.
3. Words can be chosen from the vocabulary of a particular content area. For example, mathematics words might include *square, equals, pyramid, arithmetic.*

DICTIONARY

4.16 Indian Accent (Intermediate)

Objective: To provide practice in accenting the correct syllable in unfamiliar words
Materials:
    Chalkboard and chalk
    Drum made from an oatmeal box
Directions: Write nonsense words made up of familiar parts on the chalkboard. Mark the accented syllables, as shown: dog · net'able, corn'rung. Children take turns beating out the accent patterns of the words on the drum, then pronouncing the words as they beat out the patterns, and finally pronouncing the words with the correct accents without using the drum. Children may play for individual points or team points as they accurately complete all three stages of their turns.

4.17 Dictionary Detective (Intermediate)

Objective: To provide practice in decoding unfamiliar words using the dictionary's pronunciation key
Materials:
    Duplicating master
    Typewriter or pen

Directions: Prepare a sample pronunciation key and put it at the top of the page, then make up nonsense words and put them next to the key, as shown in the illustration.

Dictionary Detective Clue Sheet

Pronunciation key:		Word suspects:	
a as in cat	ō as in ōnly	1. bap	7. gōv
ā as in āge	e as in net	2. ăn	8. peb
ä as in fär	ē as in ēat	3. därp	9. frēm
i as in sit	u as in cup	4. pim	10. gug
ī as in kīte	ū as in ūse	5. stīp	11. mūp
o as in cot		6. mon	

Divide the class into two teams. Give each child a clue sheet. Ask a member of Team 1 to pronounce the first nonsense word. If the child is correct, Team 1 gets a point, and Team 2 is given a chance to pronounce the next word. If the child is incorrect, the team has followed a false clue and the other team is given two chances to pronounce the word correctly. If Team 2 members can correctly pronounce the word, they win a point for it and also get to try the next word. The team with the most points is designated as Super Sleuths.

five

Vocabulary and Comprehension

The purpose of reading is to attain an understanding of the ideas that someone has written. The attainment of understanding is a complex process, requiring the reader to comprehend such units as words, phrases, sentences, paragraphs, and whole selections.

Developing a meaning vocabulary is essential if the reader is to understand what is read. Youngsters can learn to discover the meanings of unfamiliar words through context clues, structure clues, and the dictionary. Special study of certain categories of words (homonyms, homographs, synonyms, and antonyms) may be helpful to pupils. Figurative language and idiomatic expressions deserve attention because they are abundant in reading material for youngsters.

A reader also needs to be able to comprehend written material on several different levels. Understanding ideas that are directly stated in the material involves comprehension on the literal level. Understanding ideas not directly stated but implied by the material involves comprehension at the interpretive level. Evaluation of the ideas presented involves comprehension on the critical reading level. The creative reading level is one at which the reader goes beyond the ideas actually presented.

Literal comprehension is the easiest to attain, and it is also a prerequisite for comprehension at higher levels. Literal comprehension skills include the following:

1. Identification of stated main ideas
2. Identification of details
3. Recognition of stated cause and effect relationships
4. Ability to detect sequence.

Interpretive reading, which refers to "reading between the lines," or drawing inferences, includes the following skills:

1. Drawing conclusions
2. Making generalizations
3. Recognizing the author's purpose
4. Identification of implied main ideas.

The critical reader needs a variety of skills including the following:

1. Recognizing the author's bias
2. Determining the author's qualifications
3. Determining the timeliness of the material
4. Determining the accuracy of the material
5. Determining the appropriateness of the material for the reader's needs
6. Differentiating fact from opinion (or reality from fantasy)
7. Recognizing propaganda techniques.

Creative reading is sometimes referred to as "reading beyond the lines." It involves the use of the imagination to produce new ideas based on material that has been read. Skills needed for creative reading include:

1. Understanding cause-and-effect relationships
2. Visualizing the events so vividly that the reader projects himself or herself into the story
3. Making value judgments about a character's actions
4. Using reading material to solve problems
5. Predicting outcomes

6. Elaborating on or modifying what is read
7. Using a story to stimulate new lines of thought or new written materials.

A person's past experiences greatly influence his or her ability to comprehend written materials. Readers with rich backgrounds of experience have developed concepts and meaningful vocabularies that will facilitate comprehension of written passages. Children who have not been exposed to the language patterns and concepts of a particular author may have difficulty deriving meaning from the author's writing. Obviously then, one thing that teachers can do to increase their pupils' abilities to comprehend is to provide the youngsters with many varied experiences designed to build their concepts and meaning vocabularies. Such experiences may include demonstrations, displays, field trips, and class discussions, as well as games and practice activities.

The remainder of this chapter consists of games and activities that can be used to teach and reinforce vocabulary and comprehension skills.

MEANING VOCABULARY

Using Context

5.1 Figure It Out! (Primary/Intermediate, depending on material used)

Objective: To help children determine the meanings of unfamiliar words by using context clues
Materials:
　　Duplicating master
　　Typewriter or pen
　　A series of sentences or paragraphs that contain unfamiliar words whose meanings are given or suggested by context clues, as illustrated in the worksheet that follows.

Figure It Out!

What do the underlined words in the sentences below mean?
1. When her right hand was injured, she had no trouble doing her work with her left hand because she was <u>ambidextrous</u>.
　Ambidextrous means ＿＿＿＿＿＿＿＿＿＿＿
2. He was <u>virtually</u> independent, but he did depend on his parents for advice in some matters.
　Virtually means ＿＿＿＿＿＿＿＿＿＿＿

3. An <u>indigenous</u> plant is one that grows naturally in a country.
Indigenous means _____

4. She is a <u>skeptic</u>, a person who questions things that others tend to accept.
Skeptic means _____

Directions: Distribute copies of the worksheet to the students. Let them compete to see who can be the first to supply the correct answers.

Variations:

1. Change the activity by drawing all the words from one content area, such as science, mathematics, art.
2. Do the activity orally, asking the students to explain the reasoning behind their answers and the context clues that helped them.

Using Structural Analysis

Presto-Chango Prefixes (Intermediate)   **5.2**

Objective: To help children recognize the change in meaning of some words when certain prefixes are added

Materials:

36 unlined 3 × 5 inch index cards
Felt-tip pen
Root words written on 20 index cards. Sample root words—*happy, reliable, possible, moral, passable, mature, considerate, competent, satisfied, similar, please*
The prefixes *un-, im-, in-,* and *dis-* written on 12 index cards, with each prefix repeated on three cards

Directions: Two to four players may play. Place the root-word index cards in a stack face-down on a table. Shuffle the prefix index cards and place them in a stack face-down beside the first stack. To play, the first player turns over the top prefix card. Then he or she turns over the top root-word card. If the player can combine these cards to make a word, he or she does so, pronounces the word, and defines it. The player gets one point for a correct pronunciation of a real word formed and one point for a correct definition. If the player scores two points, he or she is given a chance to turn over another root-word card and try for a second word. The turn continues until the player fails to score two points on a root word. The next player repeats the process. If the root-word cards are exhausted, reshuffle and use them again. The game ends when the prefix cards are exhausted.

Using the Dictionary

5.3 Silly Questions (Intermediate)

Objective: To provide practice in using the dictionary to determine word meaning

Materials:
- A dictionary for each player
- Duplicating master
- Typewriter or pen
- A handout sheet containing questions similar to the ones on the worksheet that follows:

Silly Questions

Directions: Answer each of the questions with either "yes" or "no." Each time you answer "no," give a reason.

1. Is an optometrist a person who takes the most cheerful view of situations?
2. Is a ligature used in surgery?
3. Is a connoisseur an expert of some special kind?
4. Is a rudiment a person who is impolite?
5. Could a child throw a tantalum?
6. Is a valence usually made of cloth?

Special Categories of Words

5.4 Homonym Hunt (Intermediate)

Objective: To provide practice in recognition of homonyms

Materials:
- Chalkboard and chalk
- Dictionaries (enough for every student)
- Write the following words on the chalkboard

to	blue	made	right
see	plain	bear	eight
fair	sew	red	scene

Directions: Have the children locate homonyms for the words listed on the board, using their dictionaries if necessary. (Identical phonetic respellings indicate homonyms.) Then ask them to write a sentence containing each homonym. After they complete this list, they may search for other homonyms not on the list. Set a time limit for the hunt. Award one point for each homonym used correctly in a sentence.

Look-Alikes (Intermediate)   **5.5**

Objective: To provide practice with recognition and use of homographs

Materials:
   8 unlined 3 × 5 inch index cards
   Felt-tip pen

Directions: Write a homograph on each index card, using words such as the following: *read, wind, content, record, object, contract, live, lead.* Place the cards face down in a stack on the table. Each player in turn picks up the top card, pronounces the word one way and uses it in an appropriate sentence, and then pronounces the word a different way and uses it in another sentence. If the player correctly completes this task, he is allowed to keep the card he drew. If he cannot do so, the card is returned to the bottom of the stack. The player who accumulates the most cards is the winner.

Synonym Tree (Primary/Intermediate)   **5.6**

Objective: To help children develop awareness of words that have the same or very similar meanings

Materials:
   Sheet of white poster board
   Sheet of red poster board
   Colored felt-tip markers
   Thumb tacks
   Scissors
   Word cards, each containing a word that has many synonyms

Directions: Draw a tree on the white poster board. Cut a slot on the trunk so that a word card can be inserted. Draw apples on the red poster board and cut them out. Insert a word card in the slot on the trunk. Hang the display on the bulletin board. Place the apples, thumbtacks, and a felt-tip marker nearby.

During designated times during the day allow each student who knows a synonym for the word on the trunk of the tree to choose a blank apple, write the synonym on the apple, and thumbtack the apple to the tree. Periodically change the word on the trunk and replenish the supply of blank apples. (Children may also enjoy cutting out the apple shapes.)

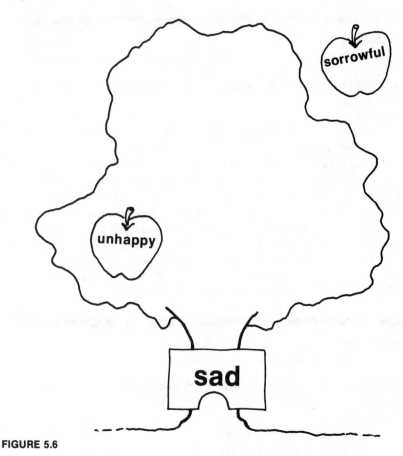

FIGURE 5.6

5.7   Antonym Flash (Primary/Intermediate)

Objective: To provide practice in recognizing words with opposite meanings

Materials:
> Unlined 3 × 5-inch index cards
> Felt-tip pens (black and red)

Directions: On one side of an index card, write a word in red. On the other side, write in black one or more antonyms for the word.

Children sit facing each other in pairs. One child holds up the index cards, one at a time, so that his partner can see the word in red. The partner tries to name an antonym for the word he sees. If he is correct, he is allowed to keep the card. If not, the card is discarded. When the deck is exhausted, the child naming the antonyms counts the cards he has won and records his total. Each time the child repeats this activity he tries to increase the number of cards he wins until he can take them all.

Acronym Antics (Intermediate)   **5.8**

Objective: To understand the meanings of acronyms better by discovering their derivations

Materials:
> Duplicating master
> Typewriter or pen
> Dictionaries

Directions: Prepare a list of acronyms, such as the following:
> radar
> snafu
> sonar
> Cobol
> NASA
> UNICEF
> NASCAR
> scuba

Distribute copies of the list to the students. Allow them to use the dictionaries to find derivations. The person who can complete the activity first with all correct answers wins. Have a class discussion about the answers.

Variation: Let students take the list home to carry out the search for derivations using parents and other resource people.

5.9   Which Meaning? (Upper primary/Intermediate)

Objective: To determine different meanings of a multiple-meaning word in varying contexts

Materials:

   Poster board (8½″ × 5½″)
   Paper fasteners
   Yarn
   Felt-tip pen

Directions: At the top of the sheet of poster board, write a multiple-meaning word. Then write different meanings of the multiple-meaning word in one column and a sentence using each of the different meanings in an opposite column. Attach paper fasteners beside each meaning and each sentence, as shown in the example that follows.

   Cut lengths of yarn long enough to reach from number 1 in the first column to number 5 in the second column with at least one inch to spare. Tie a length of yarn to each paper fastener in the first column.

   Write the answers to the activity on the back side of the card. (Answers: 1–3, 2–1, 3–4, 4–2, 5–5)

   Place the cards in a learning center with directions to the children to match each meaning with the sentence in which that meaning is used by connecting meanings and sentences with the lengths of yarn. The loose ends of the yarn can be looped around the paper fasteners. The children can self-check by looking at the keys on the backs of the cards.

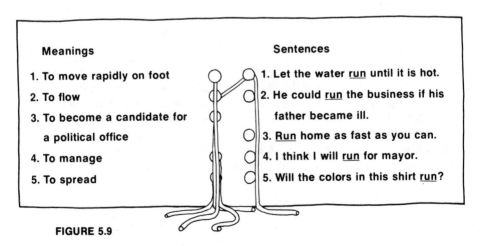

Meanings	Sentences
1. To move rapidly on foot	1. Let the water <u>run</u> until it is hot.
2. To flow	2. He could <u>run</u> the business if his
3. To become a candidate for	father became ill.
a political office	3. <u>Run</u> home as fast as you can.
4. To manage	4. I think I will <u>run</u> for mayor.
5. To spread	5. Will the colors in this shirt <u>run</u>?

FIGURE 5.9

Variations:
1. Use more sentences than definitions with more than one sentence fitting some definitions.
2. Use fewer sentences than definitions with one or more of the definitions not being a match.

Short-Fors (Primary/Intermediate)   **5.10**

Objective: To practice recognition of common abbreviations
Materials:
Unlined 3 × 5 inch file cards
Felt-tip pen
Utility knife
Poster board

Directions: Draw the picture that is shown in the illustration and title the board using the felt tip pen on poster board. Using the utility knife, cut slots for cards. Cut each index card in half. On half of these cards, write words (this is the "word" deck); on the other half, write the abbreviations for the words (this is the "short-for" deck). Write an answer key on the back of the poster board. Four children in two teams of two each participate at a time. One child in each team is the player; the other is the referee.

Shuffle the cards and place them face-down on the table. The first player takes the first card from the word deck and places it on the board in the slot on the tall figure. He or she then draws a short-for card and checks to see if it is a match. If the player thinks he or she does have a match, this card is placed in the slot in the short figure on the card. Both referees check the answer key, and a team is awarded a point if the match is correct. If the player does not have a match, the team loses a point (if it has accumulated any). If the card drawn is recognized by the player as not being a match, it is discarded into a third stack and the player can draw again. A turn continues until a player either gains or loses a point. Then the player from the other team chooses a new card from the word deck and goes through the same process. When the short-for deck has been depleted, the discards are shuffled and reused. Matched cards are removed from play. Play continues until all cards have been matched.

FIGURE 5.10

FIGURATIVE LANGUAGE AND IDIOMATIC EXPRESSIONS

5.11   What's That Again? (Intermediate)

Objective: To increase understanding of figurative language and idiomatic expressions
Materials:
    Duplicating master
    Typewriter or pen
Directions: Prepare a list of statements containing figurative language and idiomatic expressions, such as the one on the worksheet that follows. Duplicate the list and hand it to the class.

What's That Again?

1. When he heard the knock, he flew to the door.
2. When he was sick, he coughed his head off.
3. The sun smiled down upon the faces of the flowers.
4. The farmer worked like a horse.
5. He was a pillar of the church.
6. He bit off my head when I asked.
7. He was the black sheep of his family.

Divide the class into several small groups. Try to include a fairly good artist in each group. Give each group several sheets of drawing paper. Tell them to decide on the literal meaning and the figurative, or actual, meaning of each statement and then illustrate both meanings. Each group should try to illustrate all of the statements. When the teacher calls time, the children should share their illustrations and explain the reasoning behind each one.

LITERAL LEVEL

Sentence Sense

Scrambled Sentences (Primary/Intermediate)   5.12

Objective: To provide practice in constructing sensible sentences from groups of words
Materials:
Strips of paper
Pen
Scissors
Envelopes

Directions: Write sentences on strips of paper. Cut the words apart. Place the words for each sentence in their own envelope. (The words may be numbered on the back in order to allow self-checking by the children.)

Allow the children individually or in teams to choose an envelope and try to reconstruct the sentence contained in it. When the task is completed, the teacher may come to the children and listen to them read the sentences, or the children may check the sentences by the numbers on the back of the word cards or by a key located near the envelopes. Many sentences have more than one correct order for the words. The teacher should accept any correct ordering of the words, not just a particular one that he or she had in mind when the activity was constructed.

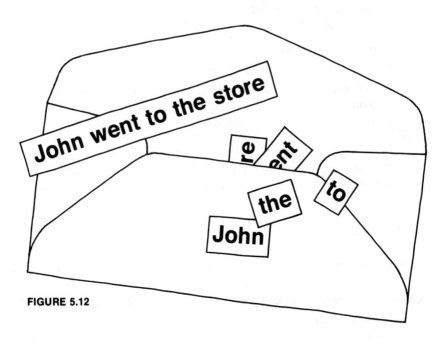

FIGURE 5.12

Main Idea

5.13 Mix and Match (Intermediate)

Objective: To help children recognize main ideas in an article
Materials:
   Newspaper articles with interesting headlines
   Scissors
   Cardboard
   Glue or transparent tape
Directions: Mount the newspaper articles on the cardboard. Cut the headlines off of the articles. Let individual children match the headlines with the appropriate articles.

Details

Detail Detectives (Primary/Intermediate) **5.14**

Objective: To provide practice in locating details in a news story
Materials:
Multiple copies of a real or a teacher-written "news story"
A list of questions about details in the story (For example: Who led the protest march? What did the leader say to the crowd? Where did the march take place? When did the march take place? Why was the protest being made, according to the article?)
Directions: Give the students copies of the news story and the list of questions. Ask them to answer each question after carefully reading the article. Discuss the answers in class.

Cause and Effect

Cause-and-Effect Worksheet (Primary/Intermediate) **5.15**

Objective: To provide practice in recognition of cause and effect relationships
Materials:
Duplicating master
Typewriter or pen
Directions: Prepare a sheet with a list of causes on one side of a page and the effects on the other side. Write the set of directions at the top.

Cause/Effect Worksheet

Directions: Find the effect that matches each of the causes listed. Place the letter of the effect in the blank beside the number of the cause.

Causes	Effects
____ 1. He fell in the lake.	a. He was breathing hard.
____ 2. He ran four blocks.	b. He felt overfed.
____ 3. He sold his car.	c. He felt very sad.
____ 4. He ate two pizzas.	d. He got wet.
____ 5. He lost his pet.	e. He collected some money.

Distribute copies of the worksheet to the children. Tell them to follow the directions at the top of the worksheet. Discuss the exercise in class after the children have all completed it. Ask for the reasoning behind the answers given.

Sequence

5.16 Who's Next? (Primary/Intermediate)

Objective: To provide practice in detecting sequence
Materials:
- Printed story
- Cardboard
- Scissors
- Tape or glue

Directions: Find a story and cut it into several parts. Cut at logical transition places in the story. Mount the story parts on cardboard.

Distribute the story parts to members of the class. Be careful not to give them out in any particular order. Tell the recipients of the story parts to read their portions of the story silently. When all participants have read their parts silently, read the title of the story and ask the pupils who has the first part of the story. The child who thinks he or she has the first part stands and reads that part orally. The class decides if the part read seems to be the beginning of the story. If it is, the child who thinks he or she has the next part of the story stands and reads that part, and so on. If a child reads a part at the wrong time, he or she must wait until the correct time and read it again.

INTERPRETIVE LEVEL

Drawing Conclusions

5.17 Riddle Challenge (Primary/Intermediate)

Objective: To provide practice in drawing conclusions from information provided

Materials:
Teacher-constructed worksheet of riddles *or*
Commercial riddle book
(If the teacher prepares a riddle sheet, it can contain traditional riddles, such as "What is black and white and read all over?," or sets of clues that are appropriate to the group of children, such as "I am an animal. I give milk. I say 'moo.' What am I?")
Directions: Distribute the riddle sheets and let the children compete to see who can correctly solve all of the riddles first, or make the riddle book available and let the children borrow it during designated times to read the riddles and check themselves on the answers.

Follow up this exercise by having children write their own riddles for their classmates to solve.

Making Generalizations

Put It Together (Intermediate)   **5.18**

Objective: To provide practice in making generalizations from data that are given
Materials:
Duplicating master
Typewriter or pen
Directions: Write a series of paragraphs from which generalizations can be made. Ask questions that lead the children to make the generalizations.

Example paragraph

All the children had the Christmas season on their minds, especially the possibility of receiving a lot of presents from Santa Claus. For a week now John had taken out the garbage without being asked to do so. Susie had been offering to dry the dishes every night after supper. Millie had picked up her toys and put them away each time she used them. Mother laughed and said, "I guess I'll have plenty of help until Christmas Day."
Do you think Mother is right about having plenty of help until Christmas Day? Why?

Distribute the worksheets to the children and ask them to read the stories and answer the questions. Discuss the reasoning behind their answers in class.

Recognizing an Author's Purpose

5.19 What's He Up To Now? (Intermediate)

Objective: To provide practice in recognizing the author's purpose
Materials:
Duplicating master
Typewriter or pen
Directions: Copy excerpts from material in which an author is trying to persuade, inform, or entertain, or assign excerpts to be read from available printed material. Number the excerpts. Make a three-columned chart for the students to use in classifying the excerpts. Duplicate the excerpts and distribute to the class, along with the charts.

What's He Up To Now?

Read the following materials. Classify them according to the author's purpose by inserting the number of the selection in the appropriate place on the chart.

    1. Read "Overturned" on page 10–11 in Super Conquests.
    2. Read the editorial "What Next?" on page 6 of the Chronicle.
    3. Read "I Surrender" on pages 52–53 of American Glimpses.

Author's Purpose Chart		
Persuade	Inform	Entertain
2	1	3

Distribute the worksheets. Tell the children they are to answer the questions by filling in the respective columns. After the children have completed the exercise, discuss the reasons for their classifications in class.

CRITICAL LEVEL

Recognizing an Author's Bias

Detecting Bias (Intermediate)   **5.20**

Objective: To give the children practice in recognizing the effect an author's bias may have on his or her writing
Materials:
Two articles on the same subject written by authors who have
opposing political, religious, or other beliefs
Directions: Tell the children that you have two articles written on the same topic. Describe the topic. Then give the children some pertinent background information about each of the authors. Ask the children, "Will these two authors feel the same way about the topic? Do you think the way they feel will influence what they write? In what way? What kinds of things do you expect Author One to say? What kinds of things do you expect Author Two to say?" After these points have been discussed, either read the articles to the children or let the children read them if enough copies are available. Follow the reading with a discussion of the accuracy of the children's predictions about what the authors would say. Bring out any evidences of bias in the articles, using concrete examples.

Determining the Author's Qualifications

What Does He or She Know? (Intermediate)   **5.21**

Objective: To give students practice in determining the author's qualifications for writing a particular book or article
Materials:
Duplicating master
Typewriter or pen
Directions: Write a series of questions such as the following:
1. Which person would be best qualified for writing about
professional football?
a. "Catfish" Hunter
b. Joe Namath

    c. "Bear" Bryant

    d. Jimmy Carter

2. Which of the following would be best qualified to write an article about making wills?

    a. a lawyer

    b. a pharmacist

    c. a funeral director

    d. a doctor

3. Would you have confidence in a book on investments in the stock market if the book were written by a car salesman? A stock broker?

Distribute the worksheets containing questions to the class members. Ask them to answer the questions and be ready to back up their choices. Discuss the answers and the reasons for the answers in class.

Determining the Timeliness of the Material

5.22 Copyright Check (Intermediate)

Objective: To provide practice in determining whether the material being read is out-of-date

Materials:

    Two books containing information about a chosen topic—one with outdated information and one with up-to-date information (Possible topics include: the moon, the countries of Africa, any disease for which a cure or new treatment has recently been discovered, any political figure who was discredited after having been highly respected.)

Directions: Read the information from the two sources to the members of the class. Ask the children why they think the information given differs in the two sources. If the children respond that one of the sources is outdated, ask how they could tell when the material was written. Let any child who volunteers locate the copyright date in each book. If the children fail to guess why the material differs, point out the copyright date in each book, explain the meaning of the date, and return to the initial question, which some students will now be able to answer. Follow up this activity by having the students check the copyright dates in each of their textbooks.

Determining the Accuracy of the Material

Is This Correct? (Intermediate)   **5.23**

Objective: To offer practice in determining the accuracy of material that is read

Materials:
  Duplicating master
  Typewriter or pen

Directions: Write or gather a series of paragraphs on a variety of topics. In some, include inaccurate information. Make some others completely accurate.

Divide the class into small groups of approximately equal ability, i.e., include some of the better students and some of the poorer students in each group. Give the groups copies of the paragraphs and ask them to do two things:

1. List sources of information that can be used to check the accuracy of the statements in each of the paragraphs.
2. Go to the library or a special section of the room where reference materials have been assembled and check the information in each paragraph against one or more sources.

After the groups have concluded the activity, they should compare their results and discuss the discrepancies they found.

Determining the Appropriateness of Material for the Reader's Needs

Research Race (Intermediate)   **5.24**

Objective: To provide practice in recognizing material that is relevant to a particular topic

Materials:
  A sheet of poster board
  Felt-tip pens
  Unlined index cards
  Buttons or other tokens for players

Directions: Draw four racing lanes on the poster board, as shown in the illustration. Put an X on the fourth space in each lane. On part of the index cards, place sources of information such as the following:

1. The "I" volume of the encyclopedia
2. An article on Cherokee living patterns
3. An article on teepees and wigwams
4. An article on religious beliefs of the Iroquois
5. The "C" volume of the encyclopedia
6. A biography of Sequoya
7. A book on Indians of the Southeast United States
8. A book on Indians of the Northeast United States
9. A book on Indians of the Plains
10. A book on Indian sign language

Write the words Source Deck on the back of each of the cards. On other index cards, place reference goals such as the following:

1. A report on types of Indian shelters
2. A report on types of Indian religions

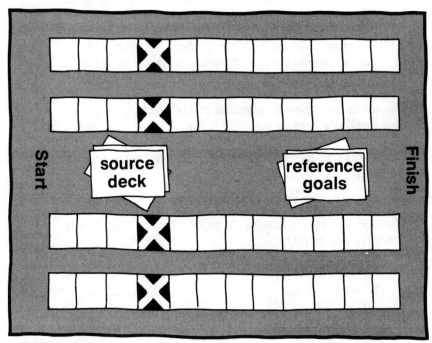

FIGURE 5.24

3. A report on ways of communication among Indian tribes
4. A report on the Cherokee Indian tribe
5. A report on the Navaho Indian tribe

Write the words *Reference Goals* on the back of each of these cards.

The Source Deck and the Reference Goals Deck are shuffled at the beginning of the game and are placed face-down on the board. A "Reference Goal" card is turned face-up to start the game. Each player, in turn, draws a "Source Deck" card and decides if the source would help to meet the reference goal that is showing. If it will, the player is allowed to move his or her token forward two spaces. If not, he or she does nothing. After each player has taken a turn, the second "Reference Goal" card is turned up, and play continues as before. After a player reaches or passes the space with the X (the fourth space), however, he or she must move back one space each time his or her source card will not help to meet the reference goal. The first player to cross the finish line wins.

Differentiating Fact From Opinion (or Reality from Fantasy)

Is That a Fact? (Intermediate) **5.25**

Objective: To provide children with practice in differentiating fact from opinion
Materials:
    Poster board
    Felt-tip pens
    Spinner
    Markers for players
    Question list
Directions: Prepare a game board similar to the one below. Make out a list of at least 100 statements, including some facts and some opinions. Label the statement with an *F* for fact and an *O* for opinion.

1. There are 60 seconds in one minute.   (F)
2. Time seems to pass quickly when you are at the beach.   (O)
3. Joe's Burgers has the best hamburgers in town.   (O)
4. Joe's Burgers has the most expensive hamburgers in town.   (F)
5. Winter is the nicest season of the year.   (O)
6. Jack Smith [a classmate] has blue eyes.   (F)

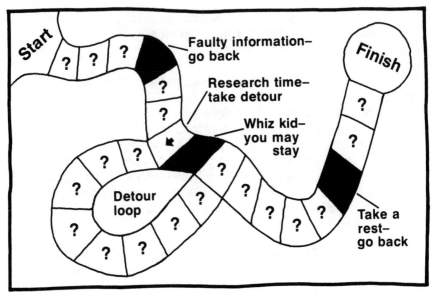

FIGURE 5.25

There may be two to four players plus one master of ceremonies. The master of ceremonies begins the game by reading a statement from the list to the first player and asking, "Is that a fact?" If the player answers correctly, he or she spins the spinner and moves his or her token the number of spaces indicated. If the player lands on a space with a question mark, the master of ceremonies asks him or her another question. A correct answer allows the player to remain on the space. An incorrect answer requires the player to return to Start. Other players take their first turn in the same manner. After the first turn, a player who misses returns to the space on which he or she was sitting at the beginning of the turn, rather than returning to Start. If a player lands on a space with special instructions, such as "Faulty Information—Go Back," he or she is not asked a question, but must follow instructions. The first player to reach Finish wins.

5.26 Real or Make Believe? (Primary)

Objective: To provide practice in discrimination between real situations and make-believe ones

Materials:

Duplicating master

Typewriter or pen

Directions: Make a list of characters or situations some which may be real and some which are definitely make-believe. Examples follow.

1. A talking dog
2. Two children and a horse
3. A purple elephant
4. A lake filled with chocolate syrup
5. A flying pig

Have the children circle the numbers of the items that are make-believe. Discuss the answers in class after the children have completed the activity.

Recognizing Propaganda Techniques

Propaganda Search (Intermediate)   **5.27**

Objective: To provide practice in recognizing common propaganda techniques
Materials:
  Eight sheets of poster board
  Felt-tip pen
  Old magazines and newspapers
  Scissors
Directions: On one poster board, write the label, "Propaganda Techniques." Cull examples from magazines and newspapers of these propaganda techniques: name calling, glittering generalities, transfer, plain folks, testimonial, bandwagon, and card stacking. On each of the other sheets of poster board, mount an example of a different technique, and label each one. Display the eight posters on the bulletin board. Discuss the definitions and examples of the various propaganda techniques with the children. Make available a large number of old magazines and newspapers and a pair of scissors for each child. Tell the children to search through the magazines and newspapers for examples of each of the propaganda techniques. The first child to locate all seven techniques displays his examples on the bulletin board, and the class checks his accuracy. If he is correct, he is declared the Super Searcher. At this point, all class members share the examples that they have found and receive feedback concerning their accuracy.

Variation: The children may conduct the search at home and construct individual propaganda posters to be displayed in the classroom.

CREATIVE LEVEL

Understanding Cause-and-Effect Relationships

5.28 What Might Have Happened? (Primary/Intermediate)

Objective: To provide practice in analyzing cause-and-effect relationships
Materials:
Passage from book containing cause-and-effect relationship
Directions: Choose a book or story that relates an obvious cause-and-effect situation. Either read the entire selection or an appropriate portion of the selection to the class, or allow the children to read the designated material for themselves. Ask the children what would be the effect on the rest of the story if a certain event had not occurred or if a different event had occurred. Here is an example from the story *Heidi:* What would have happened if Peter had not pushed Klara's wheelchair down the side of the mountain?

Visualizing Events Vividly

5.29 Word Pictures (Primary/Intermediate)

Objective: To provide practice in visualizing scenes and situations presented in written form
Materials:
Duplicating master
Typewriter or pen
Drawing paper
Pencils and crayons

Directions: Make a copy of a series of paragraphs that describe vividly scenes or situations, as follows:

The room was a beehive of activity. Mother was sitting at the table polishing the silver knives and forks. Sherry was washing the dishes while Sammy dried them and Jean put them away. Everyone was working at top speed and even Jip, the little brown cocker spaniel, felt the excitement. He ran around under everyone's feet, barking noisily.

Distribute the duplicated paragraphs, the drawing paper, and the pencils and crayons to the children. Instruct them to read each paragraph and illustrate the scene or situation described in it. When the children have finished, let them share their pictures with their classmates and see how they each visualized the same scene differently.

Making Value Judgments About Characters' Actions

Judge the Actions (Primary/Intermediate)   **5.30**

Objective: To provide practice in making value judgments about the actions of characters in written selections
Materials: A story
Directions: Read a story to the children or allow them to read it for themselves. Ask questions that will cause them to make value judgments about the actions of the characters.
Primary level example: After reading *The Little Red Hen,* ask the children if the little red hen was justified in eating all of the bread she had made and refusing to share with the other animals.
Intermediate level example: After reading *Heidi,* ask the children what they thought about Heidi's saving bread from the Sessmans' table to take back to the Grandmother.

Using Material Read to Solve Problems

Would You Have Done It? (Intermediate)   **5.31**

Objective: To make youngsters aware that some stories offer possible solutions to problems that they might face

Materials:
A book or story in which a problem is solved
Directions: Read the book or story to the children or allow them to read it for themselves. Let them discuss in class these questions:

1. What problem did the character(s) in the story face?
2. How was the problem handled?
3. Was the solution a good one?
4. What other solutions might have been found?
5. Would these solutions have been better or worse than the solution presented in the story?

Predicting Outcomes

5.32 What Will Happen Next? (Primary/Intermediate)

Objective: To provide practice in predicting outcomes based on knowledge of events in the past
Materials:
Daily newspapers for a period of approximately two months
Directions: Make the comics page of a daily newspaper available in a special area of the room each day. Tell the children to pick out a comic strip that tells a continuing story and read that strip each day. After they have followed the story line for an extended period of time, give the children time in class to write their predictions about what will happen next in the strip, based on their knowledge of past events. Let the children who wish to do so read their predictions to the class. Collect the papers and keep them for two weeks. Let the children continue to read the strips daily. Then redistribute the prediction papers. Let each child compare his prediction to the actual happenings.

Elaborating on or Modifying What is Read

5.33 There's More! (Intermediate)

Objective: To provide pupils with an opportunity to elaborate on stories they have read

Materials:

A book of fiction for each child that he or she has enjoyed

Directions: Ask each child to write another episode for his or her book, using the original characters and settings. These episodes can be shared orally in small groups of children who have read the book under consideration.

Using Stories to Stimulate New Written Products

New Ideas (Intermediate)   **5.34**

Objective: To provide an opportunity for children to use stories that they have read to stimulate creative writing

Materials:

Several stories of a particular type (for example, Indian creation myths, *Just So Stories,* tall tales)

Directions: Read one or more stories of a particular type to the children. Make available a number of other stories of the same type for the children to read themselves. After they have read many examples of a type of story, ask the children to write news stories of the same type. Discuss the common characteristics of the stories that they have read before they begin to write. When they have produced the new stories, allow them to share their stories with the class, either orally or in written form.

six

Study Skills

In order to gain information from the material that they read, children need to develop a variety of study skills. These skills include varying the rate of reading to fit the purpose and materials, locating information efficiently, organizing information effectively, reading to follow directions, and retaining ideas gleaned from reading. If pupils learn to vary their reading rates to fit the purpose for reading and the materials being used, they will be able to utilize their study time efficiently. Reading rate variation is referred to as flexibility of reading rate.

Some reading materials require careful study; some require a moderate reading rate; and others may require only skimming for the main idea or scanning for isolated facts. Thus, a rapid rate is not always the best one. As practice with increasing the rate progresses, comprehension must always be considered. If the comprehension is not high enough to meet the reader's purposes, reading at a rapid rate is useless. If the children's word attack and comprehension skills are well-developed, machines such as tachistoscopes, pacers, and controlled reading projectors may help these youngsters increase their reading rates. Timed readings can accomplish the same goal without mechanical gadgets.

Children need to be able to locate information in books, particularly in reference books such as encyclopedias, dictionaries, and atlases, and also in libraries. To locate information in books, children must be familiar with the functions of prefaces, tables of contents, indexes, appendices, glossaries, footnotes, and bibliographies.

Important skills for using special reference books include: a knowledge of alphabetical order; the ability to use guide words, cross references, and pronunciation keys; the ability to choose the appropriate meaning of a word with multiple meanings; the ability to read maps, graphs, and charts; and the ability to determine key words under which related information can be found. Many reference books are written on higher readability levels than are the materials that young readers encounter in their basal readers. Teachers should avoid assigning work in reference books that is too difficult for the students involved.

The skills needed for locating information in libraries include a knowledge of the physical arrangement of the library, the ability to use the card catalog and the *Reader's Guide to Periodical Literature,* and knowledge of the Dewey Decimal System. Teachers and librarians can cooperate to help students acquire these skills.

Children also need skills that will help them to organize the ideas they encounter in their reading. These skills are particularly important to the youngsters when they are preparing reports for content area classes. Three of the more important organizational skills are note-taking, outlining, and summarizing.

Reading to follow directions is important to children, not only in school settings, but in daily activities outside of school. They must read to follow directions for class assignments, constructing models, operating toys and other equipment (for example, stereo systems), and for many other reasons.

Retention of material read is aided by use of the skills of note-taking, outlining, and summarizing, and by reading the material critically (see chapter 5). It is also aided by discussion of the material and application of the ideas included in the material. Teachers can aid students in retaining concepts that they read about by providing the youngsters with good purpose questions.

The remainder of this chapter consists of games and activities that can be used to teach and reinforce study skills.

FLEXIBILITY OF READING RATE

6.1 Scanning Race (Intermediate)

Objective: To provide practice in locating facts rapidly

Materials:

Identical books for all of the children in the class (a textbook could be used)

A list of questions asking for facts from the text (e.g., What was the date of the signing of the Declaration of Independence?)

Directions: Ask the prepared questions, one at a time. Have the students scan the text to find each answer. The first one to locate a correct answer earns a point for himself or his team.

6.2 Timed Readings (Intermediate)

Objective: To encourage youngsters to read easy narrative material more rapidly than they have in the past.

Materials:

Reading selections with predetermined numbers of words (300–400 words)

Comprehension check for each selection used

Directions: Give the children a signal to start reading and record the starting time. Have each child record his or her own stopping time and subtract the beginning time from it to see how long it took to read the selection. Then have each one figure the number of words he or she read per minute by dividing the number of words in the selection by the amount of time that it took to read the selection. The children may be encouraged to graph their scores if the timed readings are held periodically. They should be able answer comprehension questions after they have read the selection. The comprehension scores may be graphed, too. Stress improvement in rate without undue loss in comprehension.

Which Rate? (Intermediate)   **6.3**

Objective: To give practice in recognizing an appropriate rate for a particular purpose or set of materials
Materials:
> Duplicating master
> Typewriter or pen
> List of questions such as the following:

> 1. What is a good rate for looking up a name in a telephone book?
>   a. Slow, study-type reading
>   b. Skimming
>   c. Scanning
> 2. What is a good rate for previewing a chapter before you study it?
>   a. Moderate
>   b. Skimming
>   c. Scanning
> 3. What is a good rate for reading a mathematical problem that you must work on?
>   a. Slow, study-type reading
>   b. Skimming
>   c. Scanning

Directions: Prepare question sheets and duplicate them. Distribute the worksheets to the children and instruct them to answer the questions. When the worksheets are completed, discuss the answers in class.

LOCATING INFORMATION

Books

Table of Contents (Primary/Intermediate)   **6.4**

Objective: To provide practice in using a table of contents

Materials:
>Identical books for all the children (a content area textbook could be used)
>Duplicating master
>Typewriter or pen
>Questions such as the following:

>1. On what pages would you find the chapter called "Animal Life"?
>2. On what page does the chapter called "Rocks and Minerals" begin?
>3. Does this book include a chapter on plant life?
>4. How many pages are in the chapter called "Atomic Energy"?

Directions: Prepare question sheets and duplicate them. Also make out an answer key so the students can self-check. Distribute the question sheets. Have the children answer the questions and check themselves using the answer key.

6.5 What Page Is It On? (Intermediate)

Objective: To provide the children with practice in using an index
Materials:
>Identical books for all the children (a content area textbook is excellent for this use)
>Duplicating master
>Typewriter or pen
>Questions such as the following:

>1. What is the definition of a neutron?
>2. What is an igneous rock?
>3. What is the distance from the earth to the moon?

Directions: Prepare question sheets and duplicate them. Discuss with the class the function of the index, its alphabetical arrangement, and its major headings and subheadings. Distribute the question sheets. Instruct the students to use the index to find the answers to the questions. Have them write the answer to each question, the page on which they found the answer, and any headings in the index that guided them to the correct page or pages.

Reference Books

Which Volume? (Primary/Intermediate)   **6.6**

Objective: To provide practice in choosing the correct volume of the encyclopedia to use when seeking information

Materials:
Duplicating master
Typewriter or pen
Set of encyclopedias, *or*
A poster that shows the volumes of a set of encyclopedias (see illustration)

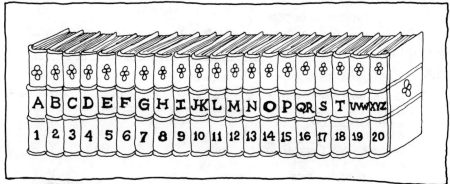

FIGURE 6.6

A worksheet with questions such as the following:
In what volume of the encyclopedia would you find information on these topics:

1. Persian cats (Volume ____)
2. John F. Kennedy (Volume ____)
3. Martin Van Buren (Volume ____)
4. United States Constitution (Volume ____)
5. Water polo (Volume ____)

Directions: Prepare worksheets and duplicate them; also prepare an answer key if you use a poster. Distribute the worksheets to the children, and tell them to refer to the set of encyclopedias or the encyclopedia poster to decide which volume contains the information. If a set of encyclopedias is used, let the children check their work by actually looking up the entries at some time during the day. If a poster is used, let the children check their answers by referring to the answer key.

6.7 Simple as ABC (Primary/Intermediate)

Objective: To provide practice in using alphabetical order
Materials:
    Duplicating master
    Typewriter or pen
    A worksheet similar to the one shown in the illustration

Worksheet

Look at each row of four words below. Circle the word in each row that would appear first in a dictionary. Underline the word in each row that would appear last in a dictionary.

Example: fat (apple) dog train

1. car   baby   horse   nap
2. cord   cent   can   city
3. sell   sail   seal   sing
4. time   tingle   tip   tin
5. every   everyday everyone everywhere

Directions: Prepare the worksheets and duplicate them; prepare an answer key. Distribute the worksheets. Tell the children to complete the activity and refer to the answer key to check their work.

6.8 Guide Words Contest (Intermediate)

Objective: To strengthen in the children the concept of the function of guide words

Materials:
Chalkboard and chalk
Directions: Write two guide words on the chalkboard (for example, *fish* and *fun*). Specify a time limit. When the start of the contest is signalled, the children try to list as many words as they can that would appear on a page containing the designated guide words. Children earn a point for each correct word and lose a point for each incorrect word. Repeat the process several times using different guide words.
Variation: For less academically gifted children, supply a list of words and then ask the children to choose the ones that belong under each set of guide words. Set a time limit. At the end of the time limit, the child with the most correctly matched words is proclaimed the winner. Several children may tie for the win. This provides more positive reinforcement than the point system does.

Code Fun (Intermediate)   **6.9**

Objective: To help children develop familiarity with the symbols in the pronunciation key of the dictionary
Materials:
Identical dictionaries for the children, *or*
A pronunciation key reproduced from a dictionary
Directions: Assign pairs of pupils to work together. Tell the children to use the pronunciation key in their dictionaries or on the handouts to write code messages to their partners. The partners exchange messages and use the pronunciation key to decode their personal messages.

Which Meaning? (Intermediate)   **6.10**

Objective: To provide practice in finding the dictionary definition that fits the context of the material being read
Materials:
A page from a dictionary available to all pupils, *or*
A handout containing a set of dictionary entries
A set of statements containing words that appear on the dictionary page with the words underlined, as shown in the example

---

Example:

run (run). 1. to move rapidly on your legs. 2. to be a candidate in an election. 3. to flow. 4. to continue.

____ 1. I'll let the water <u>run</u> until it is hot.

____ 2. This meeting is going to <u>run</u> for five hours.

____ 3. John plans to <u>run</u> for commissioner.

____ 4. I had to <u>run</u> almost a mile to give him that emergency message.

Directions: Distribute the worksheets. Tell the children to read each statement carefully and decide which dictionary definition fits the context of each statement. Have them place the number of the correct dictionary definition in the blank beside the statement number. Discuss the answers in class.

Map Reading

6.11 Map Construction (Primary/Intermediate)

Objective: To help children develop a concept of the function of a map and its component parts

Materials:

A large sheet of drawing paper

Pencils and crayons

Rulers and tape measures

Compass

Directions: Have the students construct a map of their classroom (primary) or school neighborhood (intermediate). A classroom map could show the locations of desks, aquarium, coat closets, supply cabinets, chalkboard, windows, and door. A neighborhood map could show locations of the school, playground equipment, parking lots, streets, houses, and stores. Each map should be given an appropriate title and should include a directional indicator. The students can use the compass to determine the correct orientation of this indicator. Each map should have a legend containing symbols for the objects and places represented on the map. The intermediate-level students should draw their map to an approximate scale. They may measure their strides and pace off distances to be represented on the map.

Map Journeys (Intermediate)   6.12

Objective: To provide practice in reading maps ·
Materials:
   A large road map of your state
Directions: Display the map at the front of the room. Let each child
who has taken a trip in the state come to the front, locate his or her
town, and trace the route followed on the trip. To add interest, the child
may be asked to comment on things that happened during the trip.

Which Way Is South? (Primary/Intermediate)   6.13

Objective: To familiarize the youngsters with directional indicators
on maps
Materials:
   Duplicating master
   Pen
   A variety of directional indicators, tilted in various ways, with
   north labelled on each one. Examples:

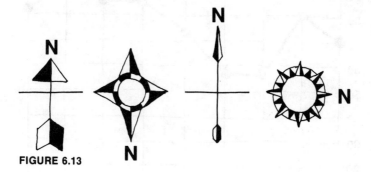

FIGURE 6.13

Directions: Prepare examples of indicators on a worksheet.
Distribute the worksheets and ask the students to fill in south,
east, and west on each indicator at the appropriate places.
Intermediate students may also be asked to locate northeast,
northwest, southeast, and southwest.

Graph Reading

___

6.14 Graph Interpretation (Primary/Intermediate)

___

Objective: To help children learn to interpret graphs of various types (pictographs, circle graphs, bar graphs, line graphs)

Materials:

Chalkboard and chalk

Directions: Draw a graph on a topic that is of interest to the class. (Vary the type to fit the levels of the students involved.) Divide the class into two teams. Ask pertinent questions about the information represented by the graph. Direct the first question to team one. If team one's representative answers correctly, team one gets a point and team two is asked a new question. If team one's representative answers incorrectly, team two has an opportunity to answer. If team

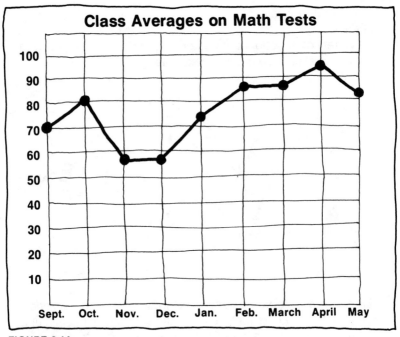

FIGURE 6.14

two's representative answers correctly, team two gets two points. If team two's representative fails to answer correctly, the teacher gives the answer and team one is given a new question. A graph is shown in the illustration.

Sample questions:

1. What is the subject of this graph?
2. In what month was the class average highest?
3. What was the class average in January?

Chart Reading

Rolling with the Flow (Intermediate)   **6.15**

Objective: To help children learn to interpret flow charts
Materials:

Chalkboard and chalk
Fake hot dogs, buns, mustard, onions, pickles, catsup (food may be constructed from cardboard, papier maché, plaster)

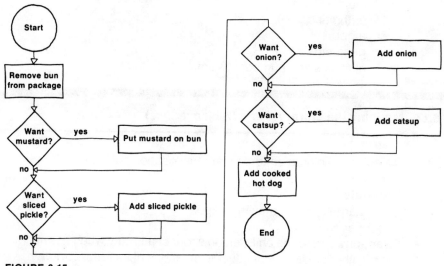

FIGURE 6.15

Directions: The teacher draws on the chalkboard a flow chart such as the one in the illustration. The children volunteer to follow the directions in the chart. Each new symbol is interpreted by a child, using the fake food, until the task is completed. The volunteer describes each decision and shows the direction of the flow.

Library Skills

6.16 Brainstorming Key Words (Intermediate)

Objective: To increase the children's awareness that information about a topic may be found under more than one heading
Materials:
    Chalkboard and chalk
Directions: Write a topic on the chalkboard (for example, mathematics). Let the students name key words under which information about the topic may be found. List all suggestions on the board. Discuss the likelihood of finding useful material under each topic after the list has been completed. An example of the key words for mathematics follows:
    mathematics
    arithmetic
    algebra
    geometry
    numbers and number systems

6.17 Mapping the Library (Primary/Intermediate)

Objective: To help children learn the locations of various library resources
Materials:
    Large sheet of drawing paper
    Pencil
Directions: Take the children on a tour of a library when it is not in use by other classes. Point out the locations of important library resources. Assist the children in drawing a map of the library which would include the card catalogue, check-out desk, reference area, bookshelves, vertical file, carrels, tables, and audiovisual equipment area.

Building a Card Catalogue (Intermediate)   **6.18**

Objective: To familiarize the students with the information available in a card catalogue

Materials:
> Unlined index cards (three for each student)
> Shoebox or other container suitable for filing the index cards
> Sample illustrations for title, author, and subject cards
> A library book for each child

Directions: Give each child a book and three index cards. Have each child use the model cards as guides and construct an author card, title card, and subject card for his or her book. After the cards have been checked for accuracy, allow each child to file his or her cards alphabetically in the designated container in order to complete a mini-card catalogue.

Card Catalogue Search (Intermediate)   **6.19**

Objective: To provide practice in use of the card catalogue

Materials:
> Card catalogue in a library

Directions: Each child chooses a topic of interest. He or she then goes to the card catalogue and looks at the subject cards for that topic. The child lists books that the library has on his or her topic of interest. The teacher can display the lists in the classroom so the children can see the books that are available in a variety of areas.

***Reader's Guide* Search** (Intermediate)   **6.20**

Objective: To provide children with practice in using the *Reader's Guide to Periodical Literature*

Materials:
> *Reader's Guide to Periodical Literature*

Directions: Each child chooses a topic of interest and then goes to the *Reader's Guide to Periodical Literature* and looks under that topic. He or she lists the articles available on the topic.

6.21 Dewey Decimal Game (Intermediate)

Objective: To help the children become familiar with the Dewey Decimal System of Classification
Materials:
A poster showing the ten major divisions of the Dewey Decimal System, along with related key numbers
Directions: Display the poster for a period of time before the game is played. To begin, challenge the children to learn the major divisions and their associated numbers. Take the chart down and designate someone to be It. He or she names a subject and calls on a child to give the key number for a book on that subject. If the child is correct, he or she becomes It and names a subject for another child. If the child is incorrect, the person who is It calls on another child. The game continues in the same manner.
Variation: In a simplified version, the chart remains on display. Otherwise, the procedure is the same.

Organizational Skills

6.22 Note-taking Practice (Intermediate)

Objective: To provide an opportunity to practice and check note-taking skills
Materials:
Multiple copies of an informational article
Teacher-prepared set of notes on the article
Directions: Direct the children to read the article and take notes about it, following note-taking guidelines shown on the next page. When they finish, let them compare their notes with a teacher-prepared set of notes on the article.

Sample Note-taking Guidelines

1. Include key words and phrases in your notes.
2. Be brief, but put down enough information so that the notes will mean something when you read them later.
3. Write the source of each note so that you can remember where the information was found. For notes from a single book or article, indicate only page numbers and make a separate note describing the source; for notes from many sources, include the title and author.
4. Copy direct quotations exactly. Be sure to show that they are direct quotations by using quotation marks.

Outlining (Intermediate)   **6.23**

Objective: To provide practice in making outlines
Materials:
    Multiple copies of an article or story
    Duplicating master
    Typewriter or pen
    A skeletal outline of the article or story (Supply main headings for several topics, as shown in the worksheet.)

Ways That Animals Defend Themselves

I. Animals that have protective coloration
  A.
  B.
  C.
  D.
II. Animals with built-in weapons
  A.
  B.
  C.
  D.

Directions: Distribute copies of the article or story and the incomplete outlines. Instruct the children to fill in the missing parts of the outline.

6.24 In a Nutshell (Intermediate)

Objective: To provide practice in writing summaries
Materials:
   Duplicating master
   Typewriter or pen
   A series of fairly lengthy paragraphs containing many details
Directions: Distribute the paragraphs to the children. Ask the children to summarize each paragraph in one sentence. Discuss the results in class.

6.25 Step-by-Step (Primary/Intermediate)

Objective: To provide practice in following written directions
Materials:
   Duplicating master
   Typewriter or pen
   Crayons or colored pencils
   Directions for drawing a picture such as the ones that follow:

Sample Directions

   You are going to draw a monster on the bottom of this page. Follow these directions carefully. First, take a black crayon and draw a circle big enough to take up most of the blank space on the page. This is the monster's head. Now give your monster two round orange eyes. Next give him a nose shaped like a triangle, with a point of the triangle toward his chin. Make the nose purple. With a red crayon (pencil) draw a semicircle for a mouth. Make the corners of the mouth turn down so the monster will look unhappy. Then color the skin of the face green.

Directions: Duplicate the directions. Distribute the sheets containing directions to the children. Also distribute crayons or colored pencils. Let the children draw the monsters and compare their products. Talk about why some pictures differ from others. Display the pictures that show evidence of correctly following directions.

seven

Content-Area Reading

Reading in the content areas presents children with more difficulties than does reading in basal readers, in part because content-area textbooks often are prepared by subject specialists rather than experts in the field of reading. Therefore, the reading levels of content-area materials are not always appropriate for the grades for which the materials were written. Teachers can check the level of any content-area textbook assigned to their classes by using any one of a number of readability formulas.

A major difficulty that children encounter when reading content-area materials is the rapid introduction of new vocabulary and concepts. Numerous new vocabulary words, representing a similar number of unfamiliar concepts, may appear throughout the text. The new concepts and words may receive little explanation and may not reappear later in the text, for the author may have rushed on to new topics. The lack of sufficient repetition makes comprehension unlikely. To reinforce the learning in content-area reading, a teacher could plan experiences such as field trips, demonstrations, and similar activities. In addition, the teacher could plan activities involving meaningful repetition of the vocabulary words in order to assure retention.

Content areas have specialized vocabularies, consisting of purely technical terms related to the areas of study and of multiple-meaning words that have special meanings in the particular content areas, that may cause problems for the students. Children may know one or more meanings for some of these words and still not be familiar with the appropriate one for the area. Figurative language and idiomatic expressions also may cause problems, especially in the area of literature.

Maps, graphs, tables, and illustrations are features in subject-matter textbooks that children need special help in interpreting. Often the information contained in these aids is lost because the children have not had instruction in their use.

Each content area presents the reader with special reading difficulties in addition to the specialized vocabularies and graphic aids already mentioned. In order to read literature with understanding, for example, youngsters need to be able to recognize and analyze plots, themes, characterizations, and sequences. They must be able to read such divergent literary forms as short stories, novels, plays, poetry, essays, biographies, and autobiographies.

Social studies materials must be read critically. Determining the timeliness of the material is especially important. Much social studies material is organized according to chronological sequence or cause-and-effect relationships, and, therefore, the ability to grasp these organizational patterns is important.

Mathematics reading requires an understanding of a different symbol system. Numerals and symbols combine with words to complicate the task of reading in this area. Abbreviations also appear frequently in mathematics materials. Story problems in mathematics books cause reading difficulties for many youngsters. In order to solve story problems, children must be able to determine what the problem asks for (reading for main ideas), determine what information is given (reading for details), determine what operations to use (reading for inferences), determine in what order to carry out the operations (reading for sequence), and estimate the reasonableness of the answer (reading critically).

Science and health materials must be read critically. As is the case with social studies materials, timeliness is extremely important. Comprehension skills that are most important in reading science materials are the abilities to make inferences, draw conclusions, recognize cause-and-effect relationships, recognize sequence, and follow directions.

The remainder of this chapter consists of games and activities that can be used to teach and reinforce reading skills needed in the content areas.

LITERATURE

Figurative Language Search (Intermediate)   **7.1**

Objective: To provide practice in locating and interpreting figures of speech
Materials:
Multiple copies of a story or poem containing many figures of speech. A sample passage follows:

> *Jane heard the knock and flew to the door. Just as she had hoped, it was Ron, with a smile a mile wide on his face.*
> *"You are as pretty as a picture," Ron told Jane as he greeted her with a bear hug. "I'm glad I didn't cash in my chips when I was in that prison they call a hospital. I would never have found out how you had blossomed while I was away from home."*
> *"It sure is great to be back. Even the house smiled at me when I came up the walk. And your smile was like the sun shining on me. I'm sure lucky to have a sister like you waiting around to welcome me back."*

Directions: Review with the class the different types of figures of speech contained in the story or poem (for example, simile, metaphor, personification, euphemism, hyperbole). Then distribute the copies of the story or poem. The children are instructed to locate as many figures of speech as they can, categorize and give a literal meaning for each one. A time limit may be set, or you may allow the children to work until everyone is finished. A child scores a point for each figure of speech located, each correct categorization, and each correct meaning. Example: worked like a horse—simile—worked hard (3 points).

Complete the Phrase (Primary/ Intermediate)   **7.2**

Objective: To help children understand the nature of similes
Materials:
Duplicating master
Typewriter or pen

A series of incomplete similes. Examples:

As white as _____ .
As black as _____ .
As sly as _____ .
Fought like a _____ .
Ate like a _____ .

Directions: Prepare worksheets and duplicate them. Distribute the worksheets to the children and instruct them to fill in the blanks. Discuss the responses in class when all children have finished.

7.3 Map the Action (Primary/Intermediate)

Objective: To help children visualize the physical arrangement of incidents within a story
Materials:
A story that the group is studying or reading for pleasure
Drawing paper
Pencil
Directions: Instruct the youngsters to study carefully the locations mentioned in the story and then to place the locations on a map to help them visualize the movement of the action in the story. For primary-level children, a folktale such as *The Three Little Pigs* may be mapped. For intermediate-level children, a book such as *Heidi* could be used.

7.4 What's the Message? (Primary/Intermediate)

Objective: To help children recognize the theme of a selection
Materials:
A story with a well-defined theme (Example at primary level: *The Little Red Hen*)
A list of possible literary themes from which the children can choose. Examples: 1. It pays to be greedy. 2. If you don't work, you don't eat. 3. Why work when someone else will do it?
Directions: Write the themes on a chalkboard. Have the students read the story, or read it to them. Ask them to look at the possible themes listed on the board and choose the one that fits the story. Discuss the children's choices in class.

Reconstruct the Story (Primary/Intermediate)   **7.5**

Objective: To help children detect sequence within a story

Materials:

Copies of the story for the children

Pictures illustrating the major happenings in the story, as illustrated

FIGURE 7.5

Directions: Make the pictures available to the children. Ask the children to read the story and then to arrange the pictures in the order in which the events occurred in the story. Number the pictures on the back for self-checking or check each child's arrangement individually.

7.6   What's He or She Like? (Primary/Intermediate)

Objective: To encourage children to analyze characters in stories
Materials:
>   Chalkboard and chalk
>   A library book for each child
>   A set of reading questions, such as the following:
>   1. What did the character look like? How old was he or she?
>   2. Did you like the character?
>   3. What did he or she do or say to make you feel that way?
>   4. Was he or she honest or dishonest?
>   5. What words or actions made you believe this?

Directions: Write the questions on a chalkboard. Have the children select books and read them. When they have finished, ask each student to choose one character from the book he or she has read and tell or write about what the character was like, using the questions as a guide.

7.7   Oral Reading of a Play (Primary/Intermediate)

Objective: To help children identify with the characters in a play
Materials:
>   Copies of a play, enough for each child

Directions: First, have the children read the play silently. Then assign a character in the play to each child in the class. There may be two or three children assigned to each part. Ask the children to study their assigned parts silently, thinking about the types of persons that their characters are. Begin the first oral reading of the play. Urge each child to read the dialogue in character. After the first reading, recast the play and have it read orally again. Continue until all children have had an opportunity to participate. After each reading of the play, discuss techniques that could have improved each performance.

7.8   Choral Reading of Poetry (Primary/Intermediate)

Objective: To lead children to the enjoyment of the interpretation of poetry through oral presentation
Materials:
>   Copies of a poem suitable in difficulty for the children involved

Directions: Read the poem to the children, or play a recording of a good speaker reading the poem. Discuss the poem with the children. Then read it or play the record several more times. Decide with the children the best choral reading arrangement for the poem: unison, refrain, dialogue, line-a-child, or line-a-choir. Assign parts to the class members and let the children read their parts, using appropriate expression. Allow the children to evaluate their own efforts and to work on polishing the performance.

SOCIAL STUDIES

Social Studies Word Puzzle (Primary/Intermediate)　　　　　**7.9**

Objective: To help children develop understanding of the meanings of words used in social studies materials
Materials:
　　Duplicating master
　　Typewriter and/or pen
　　The crossword puzzle that follows or one you create,
　　containing social studies terms
Directions: Duplicate the puzzle and key and distribute to the class.

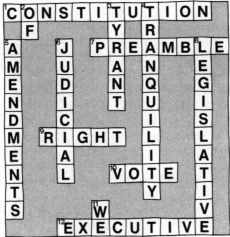

FIGURE 7.9

CLUES

Across

1. A document which was written to establish limits of government, set forth the responsibilities of the people, and set forth the rights of the people
7. The part of the Constitution that comes first
9. Something that is due to a person
10. Cast a ballot in an election
12. The branch of government that carries out laws and manages government

Down

2. Ours is a government ____ the people, by the people, and for the people
3. One who uses power in an unjust and cruel way
4. Peacefulness
5. Changes in the Constitution
6. The branch of government that interprets laws
8. The branch of government that makes laws
11. The Preamble to the Constitution begins with the words, "____ the People"

7.10 Locate It On the Map (Intermediate)

Objective: To help children visualize the physical locations of things about which they are reading

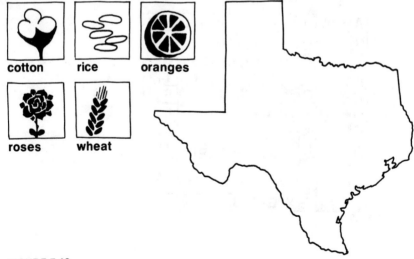

cotton   rice   oranges

roses   wheat

FIGURE 7.10

Materials:
>   Outline maps of an area under study (one for each child), as in the preceding sample:

Directions: After reading about the products of a particular area, ask the children to locate on the outline maps the areas principally known for these products. They should draw symbols on the maps to represent the products of the different areas and add the symbols to the map legend.

Draw a Graph (Primary/Intermediate)   **7.11**

Objective: To help children increase understanding of how graphs are constructed

Materials:
>   Drawing paper
>   Pencils

Directions: Have students construct a graph similar to one you wish to help them interpret in the textbook. Discuss what each part of the graph means as it is drawn. Possible types: (1) A picture graph showing the number of fish in the aquariums in various first grade classes; (2) a circle graph showing the way the children spend their day (eating, sleeping, studying, playing, etc.); (3) a bar graph showing the number of books read by the members of the class each week for several weeks; and (4) a line graph showing the daily quiz scores of one child for a week.

Reading Tables (Intermediate)   **7.12**

Objective: To help children become familiar with the arrangement of material in tables

Materials:
>   Large poster displaying a table of interest to the youngsters (for example, a table of the number of students from each class participating in various track and field events on Field Day, as shown on the next page.)

Directions: Explain the way to enter a table by finding the intersection of the correct column and row. Then ask questions that can be answered by referring to the table on the poster. Allow students to come to the front of the room to point out the correct figures. Also ask them to explain to the class how they located the figures.

	50 Meter Sprint	100 Meter Sprint	200 Meter Sprint	High Jump	Broad Jump	Triple Jump	Class Totals
Jones	7	9	4	8	15	10	53
Boyd	10	9	7	6	10	5	47
Salo	4	6	3	1	9	3	26
Trent	7	7	4	5	8	3	34
Parks	8	5	4	0	6	5	28
Lyons	11	9	6	3	10	8	47
Rains	9	6	2	4	8	7	36
Event Totals	56	51	30	27	66	41	271

FIGURE 7.12

7.13 Reading Illustrations (Primary/Intermediate)

Objective: To give children practice in obtaining information from pictures found in textbooks

Materials:
> Detailed picture in a social studies textbook
> Duplicating master
> Typewriter or pen
> Questions about the picture, such as the following:
>> What kinds of transportation did the people use?
>> Of what materials were the houses constructed?
>> How did the people dress?
>> What were some games that the children played?

Directions: Make worksheets using the questions and distribute to the class. Ask the children to study the picture in the textbook and write the answers to the questions on the worksheets. Discuss the answers in class when all children have finished.

Time Line (Intermediate)   **7.14**

Objective: To help children visualize the chronological sequence of events

Materials:
   Social studies textbooks
   Duplicating masters
   List of events culled from the books, similar to the following list
   Drawing paper
   Pen

Directions: Have each of the children construct a time line that includes all the events on the list prepared by the teacher. Display the time lines on the bulletin board.

| 1769 | 1774 | 1787 | 1804 | 1807 | 1830 | 1863 | 1893 | 1897 | 1912 |

Ⓑ Ⓐ Ⓒ Ⓔ Ⓓ Ⓕ Ⓙ Ⓗ Ⓖ Ⓘ

   A. Stagecoach service was set up between Boston and New York.
   B. James Watt patented a steam engine.
   C. John Fitch built a successful steamboat.
   D. Robert Fulton built the *Clermont*.
   E. Richard Trevithick built the first steam locomotive.
   F. Baltimore and Ohio railroad opened.
   G. Diesel engine was invented.
   H. Charles Duryea built the first gasoline-powered automobile in America.
   I. Model T Ford went into mass production.
   J. London subway was opened.
FIGURE 7.14

MATHEMATICS

Word Wonders (Intermediate)   **7.15**

Objective: To help children become acquainted with the multiple meanings of words found in mathematics textbooks

Materials:
   Dictionary for each child
   List of mathematics terms that have multiple meanings
   (Examples: set, base, multiply, difference, power, solution)
   Chalkboard and chalk

Directions: Write the mathematics terms on the chalkboard. Set a time limit for the exercise. Instruct each child to write several sentences with each of the words listed, using a different meaning of the word in each sentence. A child scores a point for each correct sentence. He or she scores two points for using the word correctly in a sentence with its mathematical meaning. The sentences cannot be simple definitions, such as "Base means————."

7.16 Math Symbol Chase (Primary/Intermediate, depending upon the symbols used)

Objective: To provide practice in recognizing the meanings of various mathematics symbols and/or numerals

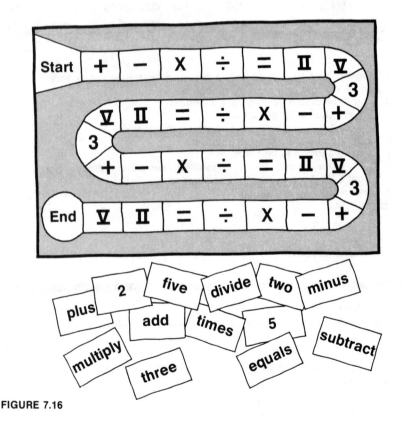

FIGURE 7.16

Materials:

> Sheet of poster board the size of a game board
> Unlined index cards
> Tokens for players
> Felt-tip marker
> Game board similar to the one shown in the illustration

Directions: On the index cards, write meanings of the symbols that appear on the board or other ways to express the symbols or numbers. Shuffle the index cards and place them face down. The first player draws a card and advances to the nearest symbol that means the same thing as the meaning on the card. If the player does not recognize the meaning, he or she is not allowed to move. If the player moves incorrectly, he or she must return to the space where the turn started. The first player to reach the end is the winner.

Abbreviation Match Up (Intermediate)   **7.17**

Objective: To help children learn the meanings of the abbreviations commonly used in mathematics materials

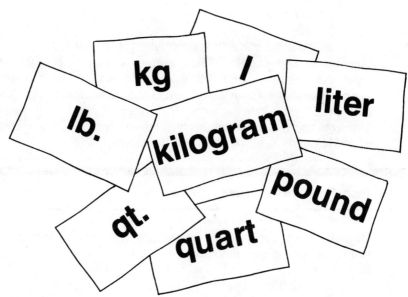

FIGURE 7.17

Materials:
> Unlined index cards
> Felt-tip pen
> On some of the index cards, write mathematical abbreviations. On the other cards, write out the word. On one card, write "No Match." Sample cards are illustrated.

Directions: The cards are shuffled and distributed to the players. The rules of the card game *Old Maid* are followed. Books consist of an abbreviation and its meaning. Books are removed from play as they are formed. The children take turns drawing cards from the other players. The "No Match" card is treated like the "Old Maid." The child left with this card loses.

7.18 Illustrate the Story Problems (Primary/Intermediate)

Objective: To provide children with one method of attack for interpreting story problems

Materials:
> Duplicating master
> Pen or typewriter
> Drawing paper
> Pencils
> Arithmetic book with appropriate story problems

Directions: Make copies of story problems and distribute them to the class. Demonstrate the solution of an arithmetic problem through the use of illustrations. Have the children read the designated problems carefully and illustrate each one. Then have the children solve the problems using the illustrations they have drawn. Discuss the results when the children are finished with the activity.

7.19 Story Problem Detective (Intermediate)

Objective: To give the children practice in logically approaching story problems in mathematics

Materials:
> Duplicating master
> Pen or typewriter
> Story problem (written by the teacher or obtained from an arithmetic book at the appropriate level), accompanied by the following set of questions:

1. What does this problem ask for?
2. What relevant information is given?
3. What operations must be used?
4. In what order must these operations be performed?
5. What is the answer?
6. Is your answer a reasonable one?

Directions: Duplicate the story problems and questions and distribute to the class. Ask the students to read each story carefully and answer the list of questions. Go over the answers in class, discussing with each student who missed the answer why an appropriate answer was not given and what answer might better have been given.

SCIENCE AND HEALTH

Word Watch (Primary/Intermediate)   **7.20**

Objective: To provide practice in recognizing words related to a specific unit in health (sample goes with unit on eyes)

A	E	Y	E	L	I	D	O
P	Y	T	E	A	R	S	P
U	E	B	E	F	I	C	H
P	L	R	Q	P	S	I	O
I	A	X	Y	Z	C	L	S
L	S	C	O	R	N	E	A
Z	H	D	W	A	O	N	G
R	E	T	I	N	A	S	N
M	S	V	O	I	P	E	L
N	P	J	U	T	T	K	M

FIGURE 7.20

Materials:
>Duplicating master
>Typewriter and/or pen
>Puzzle on preceding page:

Directions: Make copies of the puzzle and distribute to the students. Instruct the children to locate words in the puzzle related to their health unit on "The Eye" and circle the words. Tell them that the words may go across or down the page.

7.21 Build a Word (Intermediate)

Objective: To help children become familiar with prefixes, suffixes, and root words commonly found in science materials

Materials:
>Duplicating master
>Typewriter or pen
>Worksheet containing lists of word parts, such as the following: (Choose prefixes, suffixes, and roots from the children's science textbook.)

Prefix	Root	Suffix
anti-	bio	-ology
an-	geo	-ous
micro-	zoo	-ic
	eco	
	psych	
	toxin	
	hydro	
	scope	

Directions: Make duplicates of the worksheets and distribute them to the class. Instruct the children to form as many words as they can using each word part. Ask them to define each word they form. Award a point for each correctly defined word. Place a time limit on this activity. Allow the children to use the dictionary or their science books.

Can You Classify? (Primary/Intermediate)   **7.22**

Objective: To provide children with practice in classifying items into proper categories
Materials:
    Duplicating master
    Typewriter or pen
Directions: Make a worksheet as shown. At the top of the page, write the classifications to be used (plant, animal; solid, liquid, gas). At the bottom of the page, write the items to be classified (lion, daffodil; water, ice, steam). Instruct the children to place each of the terms at the bottom of the page under the correct category at the top.

Plants	Animals	Minerals

fish, tigers, daisies, rocks, grass, dogs, trees, iron, coal, cows

FIGURE 7.22

Science Sequence (Intermediate)   **7.23**

Objective: To give the children practice in determining the sequence to follow when doing an experiment and in following directions

Materials:
    Duplicating master
    Typewriter or pen
    Directions for a simple science experiment. Use the one in the
    worksheet that follows or create your own.
    Materials for the experiment: paper, metal container,
    magnifying glass, water

Science Sequence

Directions: Read the experiment. Number the steps that you must follow to
complete the experiment. Perform the experiment. Record the results.

Using the Sun's Rays to Burn Paper
    Place a piece of paper in a metal container. Use a magnifying glass to
direct the sun's rays onto the paper. Hold the magnifying glass in position until
the paper begins to smoke or actually bursts into flame. Use water to put out the
fire.

Directions: Make duplicates of the worksheet and distribute the
worksheets to the class. To get the students started, ask them to
number the steps described in the experiment. Then help the students
perform the experiment. Discuss the results.

7.24 Cause-and-Effect Search (Intermediate)

Objective: To provide practice in recognizing cause/effect relationships
Materials:
    Science textbooks
Directions: Have the students read a science unit and list all the
cause-and-effect relationships they can identify. (Example: Growing
plants in darkness causes them not to produce chlorophyll.) Discuss
their findings in class. Name the student who found the greatest
number of cause-and-effect relationships "Super Searcher."

7.25 Following Directions (Intermediate)

Objective: To help children become aware of the need to read
directions carefully

Materials:
Duplicating master
Typewriter or pen
Worksheet, either the one that follows or one you create

Following Directions

Read all of the directions before you start to carry them out. Work as quickly as you can. You have only five minutes to complete the exercise.
1. Write your name in the top, right-hand corner of the paper.
2. Turn the paper over and add 52 to 12. Write the answer here._____
3. Stand up and hop on your left foot four times.
4. Clap your hands three times.
5. Count the number of letters in this sentence. Write the answer here.

_____
6. Subtract 20 from 92. Write the answer here. _____
7. Go to the chalkboard and write your last name twice.
8. Count the number of chairs in the room. Write the answer at the top of the page under your name.
9. Write the first three words of the Preamble of the Constitution of the United States at the bottom of the page.
10. Now that you have read all of the above directions, carry out only the first one and turn your paper in to the teacher. It should have no marks other than your name on it.

Directions: Duplicate the worksheets and distribute them to the class face down. Tell the children that they must all start at the same time because the exercise is timed. When all the children have finished the activity, discuss the reasons that some people did not complete the activity correctly. Discuss the effects that such careless following of directions might have on a science experiment.

eight

Literary Appreciation—Prose and Poetry

Literature holds a special place in a reading program. Experiences with literature can expand vocabulary, stimulate the imagination, provide the sensitivity and stimulus for writing, and whet the appetite for reading.

A good literature program encourages the development of knowledge about our literary heritage, establishes skills of literary analysis, fosters reading skills, enriches the content subjects of the curriculum, and stimulates creative activities. The major goal, however, is to promote the experiencing and enjoyment of literature as a means of developing children's reading tastes and lifetime appreciation of fine reading materials.

STRATEGIES AND SOURCES

Many different procedures and activities are used to encourage children to be knowledgeable about and delighted by literature.

Oral Reading

One of the best ways of presenting literature to children is to read a poem or story to the class. A few excellent collections of children's stories and verses follow:

POETRY

Conrad Aiken, *Cats and Bats and Things with Wings.* New York: Atheneum, 1955.

May Hill Arbuthnot, comp., *Time for Poetry,* 3rd. ed. Glenview: Scott, Foresman, 1968.

John Ciardi, *You Read to Me; I'll Read to You.* Philadelphia: Lippincott, 1961.

William Cole, ed. *The Birds and the Beasts Were There.* Cleveland, Ohio: Collins, Williams, and World, 1963.

Stephen Dunning, comp., *Reflections on a Gift of Watermelon Pickle.* New York: Lothrop, Lee and Shephard, 1967.

Nancy Larrick, ed., *On City Streets.* New York: Evans, 1968.

Eve Merriam. *It Doesn't Always Have to Rhyme.* New York: Atheneum, 1964.

PROSE

Hans Christian Andersen, *The Complete Fairy Tales and Stories.* New York: Doubleday, 1974.

May Hill Arbuthnot and Mark Taylor, *Time for Old Magic.* Glenview: Scott, Foresman, 1970.

Natalie Babbit, *The Devil's Storybook.* New York: Farrar, Straus and Giroux, 1974.

Ellis Credle, *Tall Tales from the High Hills.* Nashville, Tennessee: Nelson, 1957.

Jeanne B. Hardendorff, comp., *Just One More.* Philadelphia: Lippincott, 1969.

Maria Leach, ed., *How the People Sang the Mountains Up: How and Why Stories.* New York: Viking, 1967.

Ruth Manning-Sanders, *Book of Ghosts and Goblins.* New York: Dutton, 1969.

Alice Provensen and Martin Provensen, comps., *The Provensen Book of Fairy Tales.* New York: Random House, 1971.

Ruth Sawyer, *Joy to the World: Christmas Legends.* Boston: Little Brown, 1966.

Jane Yolen, *The Girl Who Cried Flowers and Other Tales.* New York: T. Y. Crowell, 1974.

Free Silent Reading

Frequent opportunities for free silent reading should be provided.

Recreational Reading

Recreational reading involves the introduction to new reading materials and a time for reading and sharing them.

Close Reading and Study of Literature

To increase the appreciation of literature, some analysis is necessary—that is, systematic inquiry into some of the worthwhile literature read by children. Elementary children can study genre, plot, setting, theme, characterization, style, format, and comparison of stories or poems.

Storytelling and Drama

Children enjoy listening to a story if it stimulates their imaginations and depicts experiences they can understand. Literature can serve as a basis for the dramatic process by involving: (a) sense awareness (sensitivity to sound, smell, taste, touch, feel); (b) movement (body actions); (c) characterization ("being" an animal or another person); (d) improvisation (acting without a script); and (e) dramatization (dramatizing parts of stories, books, or poems).

Book Clubs, Paperbacks, Magazines, and Newspapers

Each of these creates an added stimulus for children to try out new material.

Children's paperbacks, such as are listed in the *Elementary Paperback Catalog,* Grades K–8, E, and R (Development Company, Vandalia Road, Jacksonville, IL 62650) and paperback bookclubs, such as the following, are useful:

Archway Paperback, Washington Square Press, New York, NY 10020.
Catholic Children's Book Club, 260 Summit Ave., St. Paul, MN 55102
Scholastic Book Clubs, Englewood Cliffs, NJ 07632.
Weekly Reader Children's Book Clubs, Education Center, Columbus, Ohio 43216.
Young Readers of America (Division of the Book-of-the-Month Club, 345 Hudson St., New York, NY 10014.

Consider using magazines and newspapers cited in Laura K. Martin's *Magazines for School Libraries* (New York: H. W. Wilson Co., 1941). Some favorites include *Cricket, Ebony, Jr., Jack and Jill,* and *National Geographic World.*

Films and Filmstrips

The content of films, such as *Black Beauty,* can awaken the child to the world of human experiences and values. Useful listings of visual material may be found in catalogs from:

Miller-Brody Productions, 342 Madison Ave., New York 10017
Weston Woods Studio, Weston, Conn. 06833

Tapes and Records

Many tapes, records, and cassettes are available. A few resources include:

Landmark Book Series—Enrichment Teaching Materials, 246 Fifth Ave., New York 10001
Newbery Award Stories—Learning Arts, P. O. Box 917, Wichita, Kansas 67201
Literature Recordings—Spoken Arts Records, 59 Locust Ave., New Rochelle, New York 10801
Songs, Folktales, Poetry—Folkways/Scholastic Records, 50 W. 44th St., New York 10036

Literature Response Stations

An area within the classroom called a response station or center may be established at various times. It is a place where children may plan for various modes of response to the literature experienced through mural painting, construction of dioramas or peep boxes, clay modeling, bulletin board displays, mobiles, and wall hangings. Reading can lead to many creative avenues—book discussions, panel discussions, writing imaginary diaries or letters of leading characters, pantomiming, writing advertisements, and holding puppet shows, to name only a few.

Curricular Areas

Collections of trade books can be used to supplement and enrich instruction in each of the content areas.

Reference sources also exist that cite literature to be used to enrich content areas, such as:

Hiliary J. Deason, comp., *The AAAS Science Booklist for Children,* 2nd ed. Washington, D.C.: American Association for the Advancement of Science, 1963.
Clarence Hargrove, *The Elementary and Junior High School Mathematics Library.* Washington, D.C.: National Council of Teachers of Mathematics, 1975.

Helen Huus, *Children's Books To Enrich the Social Studies.* Washington, D.C.: National Council for the Social Studies, 1966.
Kenneth Marantz, ed., *A Bibliography of Children's Art Literature.* Washington, D.C.: National Education Association, 1965.
Seymour Metzner, *American History in Juvenile Books.* New York: H. W. Wilson, 1966.
Ruth Tooze and Beatrice P. Krone, *Literature and Music as Resources for Social Studies.* Englewood Cliffs, NJ: Prentice-Hall, 1965.

Additional Resources

Resources such as the following can be helpful in providing literature experiences on special subjects:

Consider using books for beginning readers, such as those cited by Elizabeth Guilfoile, *Books for Beginning Readers* (Urbana, IL; National Council of Teachers of English, 1962) or books about special groups, such as those cited by Virginia Reid, *Reading Ladders for Human Relations,* 5th ed. (Urbana, IL; National Council of Teachers of English, 1972).

A few collections of works on special groups include:

BLACKS
Gwendolyn Brooks, *Bronzeville Boys and Girls.* New York: Harper and Brothers, 1956.
Paul Lawrence Dunbar, *The Complete Poems of Paul Lawrence Dunbar.* New York: Dodd, 1913.
Langston Hughes, *Selected Poems of Langston Hughes.* New York: Knopf, 1959.

AMERICAN INDIANS
Margot Astrov, ed., *American Indian Prose and Poetry: An Anthology.* New York: John Day, 1972.

CHINESE AND JAPANESE
Richard Lewis, ed., *The Moment of Wonder: A Collection of Chinese and Japanese Poetry.* New York: Dial, 1963.

ESKIMO
Richard Lewis, ed., *I Breathe a New Song: Poems of the Eskimo.* New York: Simon and Schuster, 1971.

JEWS
Gerald Friedlander, ed., *Treasury of Jewish Fables.* Oceanside, NY: Blue Star Book Co., 1971.

SPANISH-AMERICANS
Seymour Resnick, *Spanish-American Poetry: A Bilingual Selection.* New York: Harvey House, 1964.

APPALACHIANS
May Justus, *The Complete Peddler's Pack*. Knoxville, Tenn.: University of
Tennessee Press, 1967.

CITY DWELLERS
Lee Bennett Hopkins, ed., *The City Spreads Its Wings*. New York: Watts,
1970.
Nancy Larrick, ed., *I Heard a Scream in the Street; Poetry by Young
People in the City*. New York: M. Evans, 1970.

Packaged literature kits, such as *Owl Books* (New York: Holt
Rinehart, and Winston, 1965) should not be overlooked.
Guides to children's reading for parents follow:

May Hill Arbuthnot. *Children's Reading in the Home*. Glenview, IL: Scott,
Foresman, 1969.
Nancy Larrick. *A Parent's Guide to Children's Reading,* 5th ed. New York:
Doubleday, 1976.

Textbook materials developed for the elementary school literature
program can be useful classroom tools. One type of material presents short
selections from longer works. Its purpose is to promote an interest in reading the work and to develop analytical skills. Other books, called literary
readers, also contain short stories, poems, and selections from longer
works. An example of the latter is the *Field Literature Program* (San Francisco: Field Educational Publications, 1971). Some reading programs include a complete work of literature in the basic reader or in supplementary
books. Prepackaged sets of hardback or softback tradebooks are also
available, such as *Invitations to Story Time and to Personal Reading*
(Glenview, Illinois: Scott, Foresman, 1966).
The remainder of this chapter is devoted to activities to stimulate
reading on the part of children and to encourage them to reflect on the
pleasures they have gained from their past reading. They are centered on
reinforcing a child's knowledge of poetry, folk tales, fairy tales, fables, and
characteristics of stories (plots, settings, titles, authors, and characters).

TYPES OF LITERATURE

Can You Tell About These? (Primary)   **8.1**

Objective: To encourage recall of Mother Goose rhymes
Materials:
        Slips of paper with titles of nursery rhymes
        Decorated box

Directions: The child picks a title from the box and either says the rhyme or tells something about it.
Variation:
> Besides using Mother Goose rhymes, children's stories such as "Jack and the Beanstalk," "Little Red Riding Hood," or "Snow White" could be used.

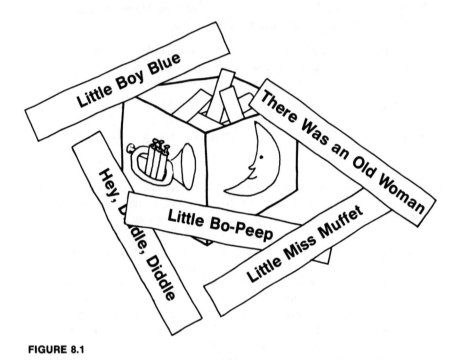

FIGURE 8.1

8.2   Can You Classify? (Intermediate)

Objective: To reinforce children's knowledge of the various genres of literature.
Materials:
> Chart, labeled as illustrated
> Box
> Index cards containing titles such as:
> *The Snowy Day* (picture)
> *Old Yeller* (modern fiction)

Stone Soup (folk tale)
"Town Mouse and Country Mouse" (fable)
"The Ugly Duckling" (fairy tale)
America's Abraham Lincoln (biography)
"Jason's Search for the Golden Fleece" (myth)
Little House in the Big Woods (historical fiction)

Directions: Ask each child to work with a partner. The children take turns drawing the cards from the box and correctly placing them in the holders on the chart. A folded answer sheet is placed in the box for checking answers upon completion.

Variation:

To help the child become better acquainted with the various genres which were misclassified assign several of these books to be read by the child.

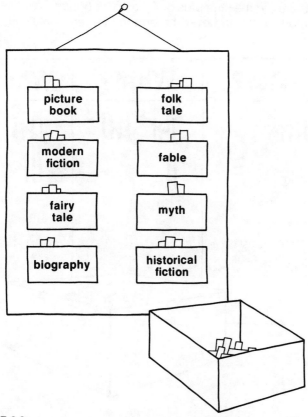

FIGURE 8.2

COMPONENTS OF FICTION

8.3   Who, What, Where? (Primary)

Objective: To reinforce children's knowledge of plot, character, and setting of folk and fairy tales.

Materials:
> Poster, as illustrated:
> Slips of paper, in a box, with such questions as the following.
> (Prepare the same number of questions for each category.
> Write answers on back so children can self-check.)
>> Who climbed the beanstalk? (Jack)
>> What was the first little pig's house made of? (Straw)
>> Where did the little pigs go for a walk? (Woods)
>> Who trip-trapped over the bridge? (Three Billy Goats Gruff)

Who?	What?	Where?
̶H̶H̶ I	̶H̶H̶ ̶H̶H̶ II	̶H̶H̶ ̶H̶H̶ III

FIGURE 8.3

What was in the house that Jack built? (A crooked dog)
Where was Little Red Riding Hood going when she met a wolf?
(Grandmother's house)
Who awakened Sleeping Beauty from her sleep? (Prince)
What did Rumpelstilskin want in payment for spinning straw
into gold? (Baby)
Where did the Prince go to see Rapunzel? (Tower)
Who caught the gingerbread boy and ate him up? (Wolf)
What did the ugly duckling grow up to be? (Swan)
Where did the wicked queen send Snow White? (Woods)

Directions: Divide children into Teams A, B, C—a "who" team, a
"what" team, and a "where" team. Pull questions from the box and ask
them of the appropriate teams. If the correct answer is given, record it
in the proper column. The team with the most correct responses at the
conclusion of the activity wins the game.

Variation:
The same types of questions could be developed and used for
modern stories.

Match Game (Intermediate)　　　　　　　　　　　　　　　　　**8.4**

Objective: To provide practice in associating characters with books
or stories.

Materials:
Several blank response cards (for writing the name of the
character)
Marking pens
Descriptive phrases of story characters:
Went underground. (Alice)
A pioneer tomboy. (Caddie Woodlawn)
Lived in orphanage with eleven other girls. (Madeline)
Slept for a long time. (Sleeping Beauty)
Lived in a bottle. (Tom Thumb)
Penrod's best friend. (Sam)
Rode to give folks a warning. (Paul Revere)
Name of a cable car. (Maybelle)
A famous spider who had a web. (Charlotte)
Lived in Switzerland with grandfather. (Heidi)
King with a golden touch. (Midas)

> Huck Finn's friend. (Tom Sawyer)
> First name is "Curious". (George)
> Billy's horse. (Blaze)

Directions: Six students are selected—three on each team. Team members sit together, and the players face the class. Both teams are given a descriptive phrase about a character in a story, and each team member attempts to write the name of the character. Upon disclosure of the responses (one at a time) each team is awarded 5 points for every match made by the members of the team. The team with the highest total at the end of a predetermined number of statements, or the team that first reaches a predetermined total of points, wins the game.

POETRY

8.5 **Poetry Tree** (Primary)

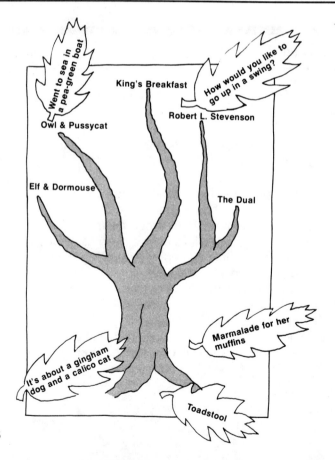

FIGURE 8.5

Objective: To help children associate incidents recorded in familiar poems with the titles or authors of the poems
Materials:
A large poster tree, as shown in the illustration
Leaves on which are written clues from poems
Directions: Explain that the "leaves" that belong to the branches have fallen off and the students must put them where they belong
Variations:
1. Use the same strategy for stories, using the title and an incident from the story.
2. Use the main characters from stories with titles.
3. Use the authors of stories with the titles.

Poet's Card Game (Intermediate)   **8.6**

Objective: To provide children with practice in associating poem and poet
Materials:
Twelve index cards per participant—half with poem titles written on them, and the others with the names of poets, as shown in examples that follow:

Poets	Titles (in matching order of poets)
Dorothy Aldis	"Snow"
Walter De La Mare	"Tired Tim"
Eleanor Farjeon	"The Night Will Never Stay"
Aileen Fisher	"Skins"
Langston Hughes	"Dreams"
Myra Cohn Livingston	"Whispers"
A. A. Milne	"The King's Breakfast"
James S. Tippett	"Ferry Boats"
Harry Behn	"The New Little Boy"
Gwendolyn Brooks	"Otto"
Paul Lawrence Dunbar	"Mother to Son"
Karla Kuskin	"Spring"
David McCord	"Picket Fence"
Elizabeth Maddox Roberts	"Water Noises"
Rosemary and	"Indian" (or "Abraham Lincoln")
Stephen Vincent Benet	
Elizabeth Coatsworth	"Morning and Afternoon"
Rachel Field	"Doorbells"
Rose Fyleman	"Mice"

Vachel Lindsay	"The Mysterious Cat"
Eve Merriam	"Thumbprint"
Mary O'Neill	"What is Red?"
Robert Louis Stevenson	"The Swing"
Robert Browning	"The Pied Piper of Hamlin"
Carl Sandburg	"Fog"
Robert Frost	"Stopping by Woods on a Snowy Evening"

Directions: Give cards to the players. When one child holds up a title card, the child with the matching author card holds it up.
Variation:
Make a pack of cards, consisting of sets of three poem title cards and a matching poet card. Deal four cards to each player. Children take turns drawing cards from the deck and discarding until they hold in their hands three matching title cards and a poet card.

AUTHORS AND TITLES

8.7 Get Home! (Primary)

Objective: To review authors, titles, characters, and episodes in a number of books
Materials:
Spinner, labelled as shown in illustration

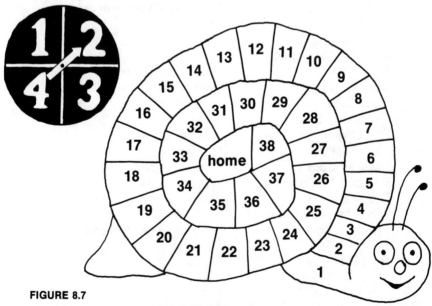

FIGURE 8.7

39-station board, as illustrated

Markers (one for each player)

Pack of cards, with literature questions on them, such as:

1. With what animal is Mr. Popper associated? (Penguin)
2. What object is associated with Mike Mulligan? (Steam shovel)
3. What grew longer every time Pinocchio told a lie? (His nose)
4. In what city did the family of ducks in *Make Way for Ducklings* live? (Boston)
5. What animal is in *Petunia?* (Pig)
6. What is *Little Toot?* (Tugboat)
7. What is *Curious George?* (Monkey)
8. What is *Winnie-the-Pooh?* (Stuffed bear)
9. Who said "I think I can, I think I can"? (Little Engine)
10. Who stole some caps in *Caps for Sale?* (Monkeys)
11. What is the main character in *Horton Hatches the Egg?* (Elephant)
12. What is Ferdinand? (Bull)
13. Where did Madeline live? (Paris)
14. Where does the story of *The Snowy Day* take place? (City)
15. Where were the wild things that Max saw? (Imaginary island)

Directions: The game is played by twirling the spinner to determine the number of squares a player can move if a question is answered correctly. The player draws a card and tries to answer the question on it. If wrong, he or she cannot move. The game continues until one player reaches Home.

Variation:

Instead of questions, the following types of puzzles could be used:

Part-titles: *The Cat in the* _____ .

Rearrange letters for title: psac ofr aesl/(*Caps for Sale*)

Complete: _____ (an old woman) lived in a shoe.

Make a Hit! (Intermediate)   **8.8**

Objective: To provide review of authors, poem and story titles, and characters

Materials:

Markers

A drawing of a baseball diamond, labelled as shown in illustration (use poster board or draw on the chalkboard):

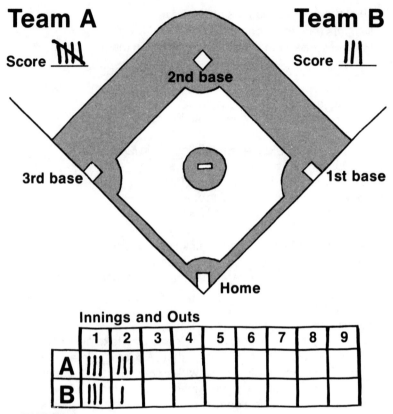

FIGURE 8.8

Materials:

Sample questions on four levels of difficulty as follows:

> *Single*
> In what book is Harriet Welsch a character? (*Harriet The Spy*)
> In what book is Old Stormie a character? (*Old Stormalong*)
> *Double*
> In what book is Mary Call Luther a character? (*Where the Lilies Bloom*)
> In what book is Julie Trelling a character? (*Up a Road Slowly*)
> *Triple*
> Who wrote *Lentil?* (Robert McCloskey)
> Who wrote *Rabbit Hill?* (Robert Lawson)
> Who wrote the poem "Lone Dog"? (Eleanor Farjeon)
> *Home run*
> Who wrote *And Now Miguel?* (Joseph Krumgold)
> Who wrote *Strawberry Girl?* (Lois Lenski)
> Who wrote the poem "Skyscraper"? (Rachel Field)

Directions: Divide the class or group into Team A and Team B. As a batter comes up, he tells the "pitcher" (teacher or student) that he wants either a "single," "double," "triple," or "home run" question. If the question is correctly answered, the batter advances to the base selected, which is appropriately marked. If the question is incorrectly answered, the student makes an out for his team. The activity proceeds until a predetermined number of innings have been played and one team wins.

Variations:
1. A consequence rather than a selection may be provided by having the batter draw a slip of paper from a box. Slips would read "Single," "Double," "Triple," and "Home Run."
2. Questions need not be of varying difficulty if each is considered a single base hit.

POETRY AND PROSE COMPOSITION

Write a Poem (Primary/Intermediate)   8.9

Objective: To help children compose rhyme or structured arrangements

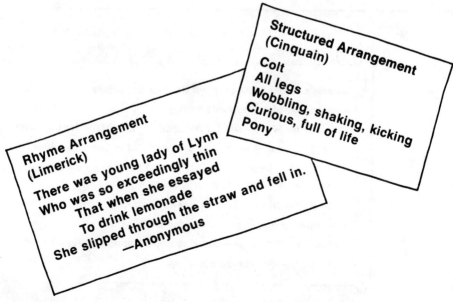

Structured Arrangement
(Cinquain)
Colt
All legs
Wobbling, shaking, kicking
Curious, full of life
Pony

Rhyme Arrangement
(Limerick)
There was young lady of Lynn
Who was so exceedingly thin
That when she essayed
To drink lemonade
She slipped through the straw and fell in.
—Anonymous

FIGURE 8.9

Materials:
>Paper and pencils for students
>Poster board on which is written a rhyme arrangement (couplet, triplet, quatrain, or limerick) or a structured arrangement (haiku, lanterne, septolet, cinquain, tanka) illustrated in Figure 8.9.

Directions: Explain the rhyme pattern for the limerick: a–a–b–b–a. Three metrical beats are observed in lines 1, 2, and 5; and two beats in lines 3 and 4.

>Explain the pattern for the cinquain: first line, one word giving the title; second line, two words describing the title; third line, three words expressing an action; fourth line, four words expressing a feeling; fifth line, another word for the title.

>Ask each of the children to write a poem in one of the two forms just described.

Variation:
>After several rhyme and structured arrangements have been written by the children, give each child cards with the name of one type of arrangement written on each card. As various rhyme and structured arrangements are read aloud, children hold up the appropriate cards.

8.10 Write a Story (Primary/Intermediate)

Objective: To help children compose parts of a story

>*Paddle to the Sea*—suggest another adventure
>
>*Aesop's Fables*—try fable writing
>
>*Whistle for Willie*—what if Peter could not whistle for the dog?
>
>*Just So Stories*—write your own account of "why" or "how"
>
>*Summer Diary*—write the text for this book
>
>*Paul Bunyon*—write your own tall tale
>
>*When I am Big*—write a "someday" story
>
>*Summer of the Swans*—describe Sara
>
>*Pippi Longstocking*—what else could happen to Pippi?
>
>*Life Story*—write an autobiography

FIGURE 8.10

Materials:
A bulletin board display of book titles, with suggestions for students (see preceding page).

Directions: Explain that these are books that have been read by a number of class members and that they can serve as a foundation for composing stories. Let individuals chose their own assignments, or permit small groups to work together.

Variations:

1. Read a story to the class, but stop before reading the end and ask, "What do you think is going to happen? Let's write our own ending."
2. Different beginnings, different endings, changing characters, and changing locales—all provide similar opportunities for written expression.
3. Use a display of a set of book jackets to serve as starters for the stories.
4. After reading the poems by Mary O'Neill in *Hailstones and Halibut Bones* (NY: Doubleday and Co., 1961) some children might like to try their hands at writing similar poems. A few representative books of stories and poems that some teachers have found useful for patterned writing are:

Aiken, Conrad. *Cats and Bats and Things with Wings*. New York: Atheneum, 1965.

Cameron, Polly. *"I Can't," Said the Ant*. New York: Scholastic Book Services, Inc., 1969.

Donamska, Janina. *If All the Seas Were One Sea*. New York: Macmillan, 1971.

Emberley, Edward. *The Wing of a Flea*. Boston: Little, Brown, 1961.

Jacobs, Leland B. *Poetry for Chuckles and Grins*. Champaign, IL: Garrard, 1969.

Kraus, Robert. *Whose Mouse Are You?* New York: Macmillan, 1970.

Oppenheim, Joan. *Have You Seen Trees?* New York: Young Scott Books, 1967.

Sullivan, Joan. *Round is a Pancake*. New York: Holt, Rinehart and Winston, 1967.

nine

Oral Reading and Drama

Oral reading has several important functions.

It can present information. A person may wish to read orally to prove a point, provide background information, provide instructions for performing some task, make announcements, or give a speech from notes.

It can be used to entertain. A person may wish to share a story or poem, participate in a dramatic reading, or act as a narrator for a play or pantomime.

It can enhance personal enjoyment. A person may read a passage of prose or poetry aloud just to hear the beauty of the words.

Oral reading for an audience requires that a reader have an opportunity to read silently before reading orally. During the silent reading, the performer can become acquainted with the author's style, determine the author's message, and check on the correct pronunciation of unfamiliar words. If a passage is particularly difficult, a reader may need to practice it aloud in order to assure proper phrasing and intonation.

Within the classroom there are numerous opportunities for oral reading:

- Confirming an answer to a question by reading the portion of the selection in which the answer was found or by pointing out, through reading aloud, the part of a story that is funniest or saddest or that tells about a particular person, thing, or event.
- Reading a news story in which the class is interested.
- Reading background information for a topic of discussion from a reference book or tradebook.
- Sharing a poem or story (published or original).
- Reading instructions to a person or group so that they can carry them out.
- Reading for enjoyment of word sounds.
- Reading for different expressions and meanings.
- Choral reading.
- Reading the narration or parts of characters in a play.
- Reading for a class "radio" or "television" program.

Of these activities, choral reading is an especially useful activity. It helps children to develop smooth, fluent reading and to avoid word-by-word reading. It gives the children opportunities to interpret good literature. Finally, all children can participate without undue anxiety, for the mistakes of hesitant oral readers are not as obvious when a group is reading.

Use an audience whenever possible. The purpose of oral reading is to communicate with others through the reading. The audience should not have access to the material from which the performer is reading, in order to provide a true listening experience.

Oral reading requires the same basic word-identification skills and comprehension skills involved with silent reading. Additionally, oral reading also requires the skills of accurate pronunciation, clear enunciation, proper phrasing and intonation, adequate volume, appropriate rate, the ability to hold the attention of the audience, and functional eye-voice span.

Several techniques can help children develop oral reading skills. Provide the children opportunities to listen to good readers. These may be the teacher, other students, or good models available on records and tape recordings. Do *not* have children watch the text as they are listening. It is not good for developing personal eye-movement patterns.

Encourage the children to listen to tapes of their own oral reading efforts and to analyze their own performances, using such class-developed guidelines, as follow:

1. Be sure you can pronounce each word correctly before you read to an audience.
2. Say each word clearly and distinctly.

3. Pause in the right places. Pay attention to punctuation clues.

4. Emphasize important words.

5. Speak loudly enough to be easily heard.

Share with children the reading clues offered by punctuation marks and provide practice in interpreting punctuation marks in short selections.

Discuss how voice inflection helps to convey meaning. For example, explore the various ways of reading the following sentence:

"She is going" — (indicating a fact)
(denoting dislike of the idea)
(emphasizing that action will be taken)
(showing happiness about the information)

Another sentence idea: "I did not say he stole the money." By changing the stress on different words, you can get six different meanings from this set of words. Try it!

Discuss with students how to break sentences into thought units.

Give special attention to reading of poetry, since poetry is for the ear and the tongue.

Use sound teaching procedures, such as the following:

1. Use material at the children's independent reading level.

2. Prepare children for oral reading by having them read silently first.

3. As often as possible, use oral selections that are new to the audience, except for an occasional story that is well-liked by the class.

ORAL READING SOURCES

Some sources of material for oral reading instruction include the following:

Basic Reading Skills Program. Bell and Howell, 7100 McCormick Blvd., Lincolnwood.

Bill Martin's *Instant Readers.* Holt, Rinehart and Winston, 383 Madison Ave., New York, NY 10017 (Books and cassettes).

People Profiles. Teaching Resources, 100 Boylston Street, Boston, MA 02116 (Books with read-along records)

Score Reading Improvement Series. Prentice Hall, 150 White Plains Road, Tarrytown, NY 10591 (Filmstrips, books, and read-along tapes)

Story-go-Round. Noble and Noble, 1 Dag Hammarskjold Plaza, New

York, NY 10017 (Books and read-along cassettes)
Some sources of material for children to read orally include:
Aesop in the Afternoon. Albert Cullum. Citation Press, 50 West 44th
Street, New York, NY 10036
Favorite Plays for Classroom Reading. Donald D. Durrell and B. Alice
Crossley. Plays, Inc., 8 Arlington Street, Boston, MA 02116
Oral Reading and Linguistics, Book 1-6, Mildred Dawson and G.
Newman. Benefic Press, Westchester, IL 60153
Plays for Echo Reading. Donald D. Durrell and L. De Milia. Harcourt Brace
Jovanovich, New York NY 10017.
Plays for Reading Progress. John Deck and others. Educational Progress
Corporation, P.O. Box 45663, Tulsa, OK 74145
Plays: The Drama Magazine for Young People. 8 Arlington Street, Boston,
MA 02116
Scope Play Series. Scholastic Book Services, 50 West 44th Street, New
York, NY 10036
Sounds of Language Readers. Bill Martin, Jr. Holt, Rinehart and Winston,
Inc., 383 Madison Avenue, New York, NY 10017
Story Plays: Self-Directing Materials for Oral Reading. Margaret Rector
and Douglas Rector. Harcourt Brace Jovanovich, 757 Third
Avenue, New York, NY 10017.
The Tiger's Bones and Others Plays for Children. Viking Press, 757 Third
Avenue, New York, NY 10017
Thirty Plays for Classroom Reading. Donald D. Durrell and B. Alice
Crossley. Plays Inc., 8 Arlington Street, Boston, MA 02116

Two sources of activities for oral reading and drama include the following:

Speaking Aids Through the Grades. Carlsen, Ruth Kearney. Teachers
College, Columbia University: Teachers College Press, 1975.
Stage. Natalie Hutson, Stevensville, MI: Educational Service, 1968.

The remainder of this chapter is devoted to activities that promote
good oral reading.

READING DIRECTIONS

Do As I Say! (Primary)   **9.1**

Objective: To provide practice in reading directions

Materials:
> Sheet of directions for reader as illustrated
> Drawing paper and crayons for listeners

Sample Sheet of Directions

1. Begin with E. Write the letters back to A.
2. Make an F. Draw a square around it.
3. Draw a set of nine apples.
   Color four green.
   Color five red.
   Draw a circle around each apple.
4. Draw a flower. Color it red.
5. Draw a balloon. Color it orange.

Directions: Divide the class into groups, and give each group a set of directions. Have each group choose a reader. As he reads each direction, it is followed by the children in his group.

9.2 Make a Beast Picture (Intermediate)

Objective: To provide experience in reading directions
Materials:
> Sheet of directions
> Drawing paper
> Assorted crayons

Sample Direction Sheet: Draw Me—Part-by-Part

1. My head is round like a balloon. It is green.
2. I have a big square body. It is blue.
3. My head has three eyes and four ears. My ears are purple.
4. My mouth has three sharp teeth. One tooth is yellow and the other two are black.
5. I have two arms and two hands. They are red. Each hand has three fingers.
6. I have three legs and a foot for each leg. They are brown. Each foot has six toes.

Directions: Make up direction sheets such as the one suggested or let the pupils write their own. In the latter case, the child who wrote the directions may serve as reader. As the child reads his or her story, the children listen in order to follow the directions. Then they try to include as many details as they can remember. The direction sheet is read once.

Construct a Paper Fish (Primary/Intermediate)   9.3

Objective: To provide practice in reading oral directions
Materials:
> Construction paper
> Scissors
> Cardboard
> Direction Card illustrated as follows

Direction Card

1. Fold a piece of 9 × 12-inch construction paper lengthwise into equal halves.
2. Starting at the fold, on the outside, draw one half of a fish as shown.
3. While paper is still folded, take scissors and cut out the fish half.
4. Beginning approximately 1 inch from the back of the fish, cut slots along center line, approximately 1 inch deep and 1/2 inch apart.
5. Unfold the fish and insert a strip of cardboard about 2 inches shorter than the fish and 3/4 inch wide.
6. Make a hole in the top of the fish. Tie a string through the hole and hang the fish.

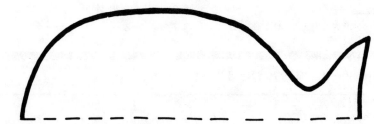

FIGURE 9.3

Directions: Make up Direction Cards such as described, or have the pupils write their own. As the directions are read by a class member, the children listen and follow them.

WORD ENJOYMENT

Tingle the Tongue (Primary)   9.4

Objective: To provide children with enjoyment in oral reading

Materials:

Copy of several tongue twisters such as the following:

A flea and a fly in a flue
Were imprisoned. Oh, what could they do?
Said the flea, "Let us fly."
Said the fly, "Let us flee."
So they flew through a flaw in the flue.

—Author unknown

She sells seashells on the seashore.
The shells she sells are seashells, I'm sure.
So if she sells seashells on the seashore,
I'm sure she sells seashore shells.

—Author unknown

Directions: Provide copies of several such tongue twisters to children. After practice, ask the children to read them aloud.

Variation:

Don't overlook good sources of tongue twisters such as:

Schwartz, Alvin. *A Twister of Twists, A Tangler of Tongues.* Philadelphia, PA: Lippincott, 1972.
———. *Witcracks—Jokes and Jests from American Folklore.* Philadelphia, PA: Lippincott, 1973.
———. *Tom Foolery—Trickery and Foolery with Words.* Philadelphia, PA: Lippincott, 1973.

9.5 Enjoying the Way It's Said (Intermediate)

Objective: To provide children with experiences in noting different language arrangements.

Materials:

Copy of several alliterative verses, such as the following:

Peter Piper picked a peck of pickled peppers.
A peck of pickled peppers Peter Piper picked.
If Peter Piper picked a peck of pickled peppers,
Where's the peck of pickled peppers Peter Piper picked?

—Author unknown

Theophilus Thistle, the successful thistle sifter,
In sifting a sieve of unsifted thistles,
Thrust three thousand thistles

Through the thick of his thumb.
Now, if Theophilus Thistle, the successful thistle sifter,
In sifting a sieve of unsifted thistles,
Thrust three thousand thistles
Through the thick of his thumb,
Beware that thou, in sifting a sieve of unsifted thistles,
Thrust not ten thousand thistles
Through the thick of thy thumb

—Author unknown

Directions: Provide copies of several such alliterative verses to children. After practice, ask them to read aloud their favorite ones.
Variations:
1. Other ways that language is used may be highlighted through reading poems that contain figures of speech and onomatopoeic words.
2. The following resources are helpful:

Emrich, Duncan. *The Nonsense Book.* New York: Four Winds Press, 1970.
Justus, May T. *The Complete Peddler's Pack: Games, Songs, Rhymes, and Riddles from Mountain Folklore.* Knoxville, TN: University of Tennessee Press, 1967.
Withers, Carl A. *Treasury of Games, Riddles, Stunts, Tricks, Tongue Twisters, Rhymes, Chanting, Singing.* New York: Grosset and Dunlap, 1969.

DIFFERENT EXPRESSIONS/MEANINGS

Show Me (Primary)   **9.6**

Objective: To provide children with opportunities for reading different kinds of sentences
Materials:
Sentences such as the following written individually on slips of paper:
Close the door, Jim.
Did you read about the exciting race?
Bill has a new red bicycle.
What a beautiful day!

Colorful box for holding the slips of paper
Set of three cards each for each pupil in the group or class,
illustrated as follows:

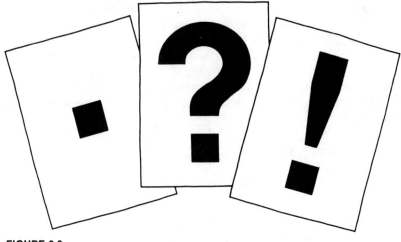

FIGURE 9.6

Directions: Divide the class into two teams. Pass out one set of
punctuation cards to each child. Have a child from Team A select a
slip of paper from the box and read the sentence with expression so
the class will know what type of sentence he or she is reading. Then
the students in Team B hold up the end punctuation mark for the
sentence read. The teacher counts the students in Team B who
answered correctly and records that number. Then a child from Team
B selects a slip of paper. After each child has had a turn, the points
are tallied and the winning team is announced.

9.7 Express it Differently (Intermediate)

Objective: To provide practice in reading sentences to convey
particular meanings
Materials:
Sets of sentences that may be read with various emphases,
such as:

Joe is my best friend. (Not Tom)
Joe *is* my best friend. (Not was)
Joe is *my* best friend. (Not someone else's)
Joe is my *best* friend. (Not second or third)
Joe is my best *friend.* (Not a book)

Directions: Provide a set of such sentences to children. Ask a child to read a sentence aloud, allowing others in the group to suggest what is *not* meant.

This activity could be played by two teams. Pass out a slip of paper, with the key word underlined, to each team member. A child from Team A reads his or her sentence. A child from the other team must respond with what is not meant. The teacher or scorekeeper records a point for a correct answer. Then the procedure is reversed. After each child has taken a turn, the points are tallied and the winning team is announced.

Variations:
1. A word such as "Oh" may be supplied to a child. He may be asked to read it as if he is hurt, then as if he is surprised.
2. Sentences may be furnished to be read in as many ways as possible to convey different meanings. Use sentences such as, "I said shut the door" or "You're a real friend."

Phrase it Right (Primary/Intermediate)   **9.8**

Objective: To focus the children's attention upon thought phrases or units

Materials:
A marked selection, duplicated for each member of the class. A sample follows:

One day / when Jim went fishing /, he found a young bird/. The young bird/had a broken wing/. Jim went to the campsite /, carrying the injured bird / in his arms /. His father was pleased / when he saw how gently / his son was treating the bird /.

Directions: A separate story is provided for each child in the group or class. The material used is written at each child's reading level. After the children have read silently and practiced the phrasing, ask each child to read aloud to his or her group or the class.

Variation:
Cut the story apart and add numerals above the
segments: "One day / when Jim was fishing, /" and so on. Ask
the children to arrange the segments in order of the numerals
and have each one read only his or her phrase or unit.

The numerals 1 and 2 appear above "One day" and "when Jim was fishing," respectively.

CHORAL READING

9.9   Choral Duet (Primary)

Objective: To provide practice with antiphonal choral reading
Materials:
Choral verse, illustrated as follows

First Voice:	Mousie, mousie, Where is your little wee housie?
Second Voice:	Here is the door Under the floor.
Together:	Said mousie, mousie.
First Voice:	Mousie, mousie, May I come into your housie?
Second Voice:	You can't get in, You have to be thin,
Together:	Said mousie, mousie.
First Voice:	Mousie, mousie, Won't you come out of your housie?
Second Voice:	I'm sorry to say I'm busy all day,
Together:	Said mousie, mousie.

—Author unknown

Directions: Pair off the children. Let them practice reading the poem,
using a tape recorder. Then let them read to the class.
Variation:
Use a verse with a refrain such as:

LEADER: *On summer mornings when it's hot*
A rider's horse can't even trot,
But pokes along like this——

ALL: *Klip-klop, klip-klop, klip-klop.*
LEADER: *But in the winter brisk*
        He perks right up and wants to frisk,
        And then he goes like this——
ALL: *Klippity-klip, klippity-klip,*
        Klippity-klip, klop, klip-klop.

—Author unknown

Variations:
1. Other examples of refrain verse include "The Wind" by Robert Lewis Stevenson for the primary years; for the intermediate years, try "Shoes and Stockings" by A. A. Milne.
2. Try line-a-child choral reading. An example of a poem suitable for this treatment in the primary years would be "The Goblin" by Rose Fyleman; for the intermediate years, "Pippa's Song" by Robert Browning.
3. Don't overlook good sources of choral reading, such as May Hill Arbuthnot and Shelton Root, *Time for Poetry* (Glenview, IL: Scott, Foresman and Co., 1968) and Marjory F. Brown-Azarowicz, *A Handbook of Creative Choral Speaking* (Minneapolis, MN: Burgess, 1970).

Say it Together (Intermediate)   **9.10**

Objective: To provide practice with unison choral reading
Materials: A verse that lends itself to unison speaking, illustrated as follows:

Monday's child is fair of face,
Tuesday's child is full of grace,
Wednesday's child is full of
    woe,
Thursday's child has far to go,
Friday's child is loving and
    giving,
Saturday's child works for its
    living,
And a child that's born on the
    Sabbath day
Is fair, and wise and good and
    gay.

—Author unknown

Directions: A group of five or six children may wish to study unison speaking of a verse. Important words to give heavy emphasis in each line may be underlined, such as "Monday's child is fair of face . . ." A tape recorder may be helpful for practice before sharing with a larger group of peers.

Variations:

1. Other examples of verse that can be treated in unison choral reading include "Poor Old Woman" and "Trains" by James Tippett for the primary years; "Roads" by Rachael Fields and "Jonathan Bing" by Beatrice Brown for the intermediate years.
2. A poem such as "Monday's Child" is also good for line-a-child or line-a-choir choral reading arrangement.

NARRATION/CHARACTER PARTS IN PLAYS

9.11 Read the Fable (Primary/Intermediate)

Objective: To provide children with experience in reading narration and character parts in play format

Materials:

A script, possibly adapted from one of Aesop's Fables, as illustrated:

The Country and the City Mouse

NARRATOR: *Far, far away in the country, there lived a poor simple mouse. Now this mouse lived in the wall of an old farmer's house. One day there was a loud knocking on the wall. This was very unusual since the Country Mouse did not get visitors very often. When he opened the hole, the Country Mouse could not believe his eyes: standing in the door was his old friend who had moved away to the city.*

CITY MOUSE: *Surprise. It's me. Bet you didn't expect to see me again.*

COUNTRY MOUSE: *No, I didn't. Come in. How are things in the city?*

CITY MOUSE: *Things couldn't be better. There's always something new to see and do in the city. How are things in the country? I bet nothing has changed since I left.*

COUNTRY
MOUSE: *Things are fine—same as usual. Let me fix you something to eat. You must be starved.*

NARRATOR: *The Country Mouse fixed a feast of bits of bacon, five green peas, and a slice of fresh cheese. After they had eaten, they sat around and talked.*

CITY
MOUSE: *I was so hungry that even that simple meal tasted good. I guess a change from roast beef and big blocks of blue cheese is good.*

COUNTRY
MOUSE: *Well, we certainly don't have any of those fancy foods here. But there is enough to eat. The air is fresh and the countryside is cool and green.*

CITY
MOUSE: *That's well and good if you like the outdoors. But I like the lobby of a big fine hotel or the sight of a tall giant skyscraper better.*

COUNTRY
MOUSE: *It does sound exciting. We certainly don't have any hotels or skyscrapers here.*

CITY
MOUSE: *Why don't you pack your suitcase and come visit me in the city?*

COUNTRY
MOUSE: *All right, let's go.*

NARRATOR: *The Country and City Mice left for the city. Now the City Mouse lived in the living room of a large, well-furnished house. The City Mouse's favorite hiding place was inside a soft, roomy couch. Inside the couch was a floor of silk shirts. The furnishing included a bar of fresh, perfumed soap and a silver cereal bowl. All of a sudden, there was a loud roaring sound. Then the silk shirt disappeared. The fresh, perfumed soap vanished next. The silver cereal bowl in which the Country Mouse was sitting started to slide toward the door. The Country Mouse jumped out of the silver cereal bowl— just in time. He grabbed and held to one of the springs in the couch.*

COUNTRY
MOUSE: *What's happening? Help, do something!*

CITY
MOUSE: *What can I do? Hold on tight. It's just the maid vacuuming.*

COUNTRY
MOUSE: *What is vacuuming?*

CITY
MOUSE: *It's kind of like sweeping. But you don't use a broom.*

COUNTRY
MOUSE: *Well, a broom can't swallow you! It's too dangerous in the city. I'm packing and going back to the country. You*

> *can have your vacuuming, silk shirts, and sweet-*
> *smelling soap. Give me an old wool blanket and a bar*
> *of lye soap any time.*

NARRATOR: *The Country Mouse went back to the country where he was*
very happy and content to spend the rest of his days—
breathing the fresh air and walking through the green
hills of the country.

Directions: Each child may choose the part he or she would.like
to read. After practice, the players present the dramatic reading to a
group of children or to the entire class.

Variations:

The children may write their own scripts rather than using a
prepared adaptation.

9.12 Radio or Television Play (Primary/Intermediate)

Objective: To provide children with experience in reading narration
and character parts for "radio" or "television"

Materials:

Script, possibly developed on the basis of a field trip to a place
of interest, such as the zoo, as shown in following sample:

A Trip to the Zoo

TEACHER: *Boys and girls, next week we will take a trip to the zoo.*
Everyone be sure to take the permit paper home. Make
sure your parents sign it.

JENNY: *Can I bring my frog along?*

TEACHER: *No, there will be plenty of animals at the zoo.*

RAMÓN: *Can I bring peanuts to feed the elephants?*

TEACHER: *No, the zookeepers don't want you to feed any of the*
animals. Each animal is on a special diet. Besides an
elephant might mistake your finger for a peanut.

CHRIS: *I'm going to bring my toy rifle along and go hunting.*

TEACHER: *Chris, the zoo is not a place where animals are hunted or*
shot. It is a place where everyone can watch the
animals and enjoy them for the special creatures that
they are.

NARRATOR: *The children arrive at the entrance to the zoo. One by one*
each boy and girl steps off the bus.

TEACHER: *Class, try to stay together. Do not run ahead. We will pass*
by every cage so just wait until we get to your favorite
animal.

JENNY: *Are we going to see any frogs?*

TEACHER: *You might. But, remember, don't try to catch any!*

CHRIS: *There's a big brown bear. He's lying on his back. I bet he's trying to get a sun tan.*

RAMÓN: *How will he know when he has a good tan?*

TEACHER: *Bears don't get tans like people do.*

CHRIS: *How about frogs? Don't they wear sunglasses?*

TEACHER: *Frogs don't get suntanned, either. The only frogs that wear sunglasses are the ones on the Saturday morning cartoons.*

RAMÓN: *Look, there's a baby elephant. Do baby elephants eat baby food?*

TEACHER: *No, they drink milk that their mother gives them.*

CHRIS: *Is it "Pet Milk"?*

TEACHER: *No it isn't. "Pet Milk" comes from a cow. The elephant's mother makes the milk inside her body.*

CHRIS: *Is it good?*

TEACHER: *Yes, it is, but it's made for baby elephants and not boys and girls. Does anyone know what animal that is?*

JENNY: *It looks like a black garden hose.*

TEACHER: *Yes it does. But a garden hose doesn't have eyes or a mouth.*

CHRIS: *Is it a worm?*

TEACHER: *No, it's a snake. Who knows what snakes like to eat?*

JENNY: *They eat frogs and mice.*

TEACHER: *Yes they do. How did you know that, Jenny?*

JENNY: *My last pet frog was eaten by a snake.*

TEACHER: *I'm sorry, but some animals are eaten by others for food.*

NARRATOR: *The children walked until they came to a tall, wide cage.*

RAMÓN: *I know what that is. It's a monkey.*

CHRIS: *And that's a cow with a fire hose on his nose.*

RAMÓN: *That's not a cow. It's an elephant.*

JENNY: *That's a deer with a long, long neck.*

TEACHER: *No, that's a giraffe. Its neck is long so it can chew the leaves off the trees. Children, it's time now to get back on the bus. Jenny, what's that moving under your shirt?*

JENNY: *It's my new frog, Fred.*

TEACHER: *Fred belongs here with all the other animals.*

JENNY: *If he stays here, the snake might eat him.*

TEACHER: *Jenny, your frog wouldn't be happy living with you. He needs to be around other animals. Say goodbye to him and let him go.*

JENNY: *Goodbye, Fred. See you next time we come to the zoo.*

TEACHER: *Everybody back on the bus. It's time to get back to school.*

RAMÓN: *Bye, baby elephant.*

CHRIS: *Bye, Mr. Giraffe. Enjoy your salad.*

NARRATOR: *The children rode back to school on the bus. That night they told their parents and brothers and sisters all about the different animals. And, oh, yes. Jenny never caught a frog again. But she went to visit Fred at the zoo as often as she could.*

Directions: Have children choose the parts they would like to read. After practice, they may present the dramatic reading to a group of children or to the entire class.

Variations:

1. The children may write their own scripts, rather than using a prepared one.
2. Such a radio "play" may be prepared and presented through the school's intercommunication system.
3. The "television" effect may be achieved by having one group of children make a videotape of the production and show it to another group of viewers.

ten

Recreational and Informational Reading

It is not enough to teach children the skills involved in reading—teachers must also focus on motivating and stimulating them to enjoy reading. Children should be helped to enjoy reading as a leisure activity and as a technique for gathering information.

One of the most important ways of helping children enjoy reading as a leisure activity is to provide reading materials related to their interests. To accomplish this, one must first determine and then expand interests of children so they will desire more and more information.

At an early age, children often begin to read all kinds of materials from newspapers, such as comics, sports reports, society news, local news, national news, foreign news, editorials, and columns. Consequently, pupils should know something about newspapers as a medium of information and entertainment. They need to know how to read and judge them. Children need help in scanning headlines, picking out main points in articles, and detecting the writer's point of view. An initial activity in the study of newspapers would be to administer a newspaper-reading survey questionnaire to a class. From this could follow developmental activities that might include locating and listing the types of materials found in newspapers, comparing various neighborhood papers, finding illustrations of stories with accurate or misleading captions, identifying the five *W*s and an *H* (where, when, why, who, what, and how) in the leading paragraphs, studying how news agencies operate, learning what a reporter does, learning about some famous cartoonists, discussing the types of illustrations used, studying the advertisements, and reading the television schedule. A visit to a newspaper might be made or a local editor might be invited to speak to the class. Concurrent with such study, some pupils may wish to publish a class newspaper. Activities required in this effort involve pupils in many aspects of the language arts.

Magazines and periodicals for elementary school children have been available for several years. Some favorites include:

American Girl. (Girl Scouts of U.S.A., 830 Third Ave., New York, NY 10022)

American Junior Red Cross News. (American Red Cross, 18th and D Streets, Washington, DC 20006)

Arizona Highways. (Arizona Highways, 2039 W. Lewis Highway, Phoenix, AZ 85009)

Audubon. (National Audubon Society, 950 Third Ave., New York, NY 10022)

Bananas. (Scholastic Magazines, 50 W. 44th St., New York, NY 10036)

The Boy's Life. (Boy Scouts of America, New Brunswick, NJ 08903)

Calling All Girls. (Parents' Institute, Inc., 52 Vanderbilt Ave., New York, NY 10017)

Child Life. (Curtis Publishing Co., 1100 Waterway Blvd., Indianapolis, IN 46206)

Children's Digest. (Parents' Magazine Press, Inc., 52 Vanderbilt Ave., New York, NY 10017)

Cricket. (Open Court Co., 1058 Eighth St., LaSalle, IL 61301)

Dynamite. (Scholastic Magazines, 50 W. 44th St., New York, NY 10036)

Ebony, Jr. (Johnson Publishing Co. Inc., 820 South Michigan Ave., Chicago, IL 60605)

Electric Company Magazine. (Children's Television Workshop, 1 Lincoln Plaza, New York, NY 10023)

Highlights for Children. (Highlights for Children, Inc., 2300 W. Fifth Ave., Columbus, OH 43216)

Humpty Dumpty Magazine. (Parents' Magazine Press, Inc., 52 Vanderbilt Ave., New York, NY 10017)

Jack and Jill. (Curtis Publishing Co., Independence Square, Philadelphia, PA 19105)

National Geographic School Bulletin. (National Geographic Society, Seventeenth and M Streets, N.W., Washington, DC 20036)

National Parks. (National Parks and Conservation Association, 1701 Eighteenth Street, N.W., Washington, DC 20096)

Natural History Magazine. (American Museum of Natural History, Central Park, West 79th St., New York, NY 10024)

Ranger Rick's Nature Magazine. (Scholastic Magazines, 50 W. 44th St., New York, NY 10036)

Supermag. (Scholastic Magazines, 50 W. 44th St., New York, NY 10036)

Wow. (Scholastic Magazines, 50 W. 44th St., New York, NY 10036)

Young World. (Saturday Evening Post Co., 1100 Waterway Blvd., P.O. Box 567 B, Indianapolis, IN 46206)

High motivation is built into cooking activities. Children can read recipes for exact meanings and then follow the sequence of ideas presented. They soon learn that not to do so will produce poor results. As a child develops interest in reading cookbooks and recipes in newspapers and magazines, his or her ability to read for specific information increases.

In their leisure time children read books that contain simple directions for making things. These books may stimulate the development of hobbies. Many times these are "how to" books on topics such as how to bind books, knit, sew, or play a sport. In the process of completing a project, they may need some special service—so they can learn to read the yellow pages in the telephone directory. Or it may be necessary to read a mail order catalogue in order to purchase some item.

Some recreational reading helps children to better understand themselves and others. Using books for this purpose is sometimes referred to as bibliotherapy. Through books on human relations, children develop positive self-images, learn to live with others, appreciate other cultures, and cope with change.

Unfortunately, children's literature is sometimes associated only with reading and other language arts areas and is dissociated from mathematics, science, social studies, art, music, health, and safety even though literature can contribute to all these curriculum areas in virtually innumerable ways.

Children read many materials in their everyday lives: TV guides, telephone books, Boy and Girl Scout manuals, catalogues, menus, travel brochures, directions for games, greeting cards, hobby materials, food and medicine containers, toy repair manuals, report cards, booklets dealing with school procedures and rules, cereal boxes, road signs, and nature guides. Much can be accomplished through such materials, especially for children who will never become proficient readers but who need to learn basic reading survival skills.

The remainder of this chapter presents activities related to the topics just described.

INTERESTS

10.1   What are Your Interests? (Primary/Intermediate)

Objective: To determine the interests of children
Materials:
Interest inventory, such as is the one illustrated

General and Reading Interest Inventory
Name: _____ Grade: _____ Age: _____
General Interests
1. What do you like to do in your free time?
2. What are your favorite TV shows?
3. What are your favorite hobbies?
4. What games or sports do you like best?
5. What clubs or other groups do you belong to?
6. Do you have any pets? If yes, what?
7. What are your favorite types of movies?
8. What is your favorite school subject?
9. What is your most disliked school subject?

Reading
1. How often do you go to the public library?
2. What are the favorite books that you own?
3. What things do you like to read about?
4. What comic books do you read?
5. What magazines do you read?
6. What are some books you have liked?
7. What part of the newspaper do you read most frequently?
8. Do you like to read?
Source: Betty D.Roe et al. Reading Instruction in the Secondary School (Chicago: Rand McNally College Publishing Co., 1976).

Directions: Ask the children to complete this form or use it as a guide for informal talks and observations about themselves.
Variation:
For interest-grouping purposes, prepare a chart such as the following one. Put a mark or notation by the child's name under his or her current interests.

Name of Pupil	Interests or Activities							
	Animals	Pets	Hobby	Games/ Sports	Comic Books	Mystery Stories	Famous People	Science

FIGURE 10.1

NEWSPAPERS

What's In the News? (Intermediate) 10.2

Objective: To provide children with opportunities to find information in the newspaper.

Materials:

Copies of newspapers, appropriate to the reading levels of the children.

Set of questions, illustrated as follows:

Activity: Use the newspaper to help you answer these questions.

1. On what page can you find sports?
2. What movie would you choose to attend?
3. What page is devoted to comics?
4. On what page can you find listings about things to buy?
5. If you had $10 to buy things, what would you buy?
6. Which restaurant would you select? Why?
7. What is your horoscope?
8. What is the least expensive moped advertised?
9. What TV programs would you like to watch tonight?
10. What is your favorite comic character in this paper?

Directions: After reading the questions aloud, let each child read the newspaper and answer the questions. The children's answers may be compared and discussed.

Variations:

1. Rather than emphasizing a general overview of the newspaper as suggested, specific focus may be directed upon a single part of the paper, for example, newspaper advertisements. A set of questions could be developed for finding information in the advertisements.
2. A set of questions could be developed for finding (a) information in the Yellow Pages; (b) information in mail-order catalogues; (c) information from transportation schedules (bus, plane, train); and (d) information from travel booklets.

MAGAZINES

10.3 Magazine Puzzle (Primary/Intermediate)

Objective: To provide children with an opportunity for recreational reading in a magazine

Materials:

Copies of children's magazines, appropriate for the reading level, containing activities for students to do

Directions: Find several seasonal or holiday activities in the magazines such as shown in the sample. These appear often in children's magazines. Let children work as pairs to complete the activities.

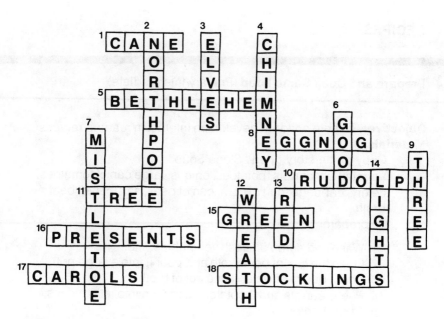

Across

1. Red and white, a candy ____.
5. Where Jesus Christ was born.
8. A drink at Christmas time.
10. Red-nosed reindeer.
11. What you hang ornaments on.
15. Color associated with Christmas time of year.
16. What you get for Christmas and Hanukkah.
17. Songs of the season.
18. Red; hung by the fireside with care.

Down

2. Where Santa lives.
3. Santa's helpers.
4. What Santa goes down to get into some people's homes.
6. What you should be in order to get gifts.
7. Plant that hangs over doors at Christmas time.
9. Number of wise men.
12. Hung on the front door this time of year.
13. The color of Rudolph's nose.
14. Christmas trees usually have many colored ____ .

FIGURE 10.3

RECIPES

━━

10.4 Prepare and Cook Some Food (Primary/Intermediate)

Objective: To help children develop an interest in reading recipes
Materials:
Copy of the story titled "Stone Soup"
Vegetables: carrots, potatoes, onions, large can of tomatoes, celery, cabbage, can of corn, can of peas, salt, can of beef broth
To prepare:

1. Wash and scrub all fresh vegetables.
2. Open the can of beef broth and pour it into a large pot.
3. Add 2 quarts of water to the pot of broth.
4. Peel 3 carrots and 3 potatoes and dice into little pieces.
5. Chop 1 onion.
6. Open can of tomatoes and add to beef broth.
7. Chop 5 celery stalks.
8. Slice ½ cabbage head.
9. Open the cans of corn and peas and add to broth.
10. Add all other vegetables to the pot. Stir well.
11. Add 1 tablespoon of salt to pot of soup and stir well.
12. Set pot on stove over high heat.
13. When soup begins to boil, reduce heat to simmer or low and cook for about 2 hours, stirring occasionally.

Directions: After reading the story "Stone Soup" to the class or group, discuss how to make the soup. Watch the children as they prepare the vegetables according to the directions. Emphasize the action words used in the recipe.
Variation:
Any number of foods are easily prepared by children if recipes are available, such as:
popcorn
applesauce
tortillas
salad

CONSTRUCTIONS

Oriental Book Binding (Primary/Intermediate)   **10.5**

Objective: To help children develop interest in construction projects

Materials:
>   10 sheets of 8½ × 11 inch white typing paper
>   2 pieces of 2 × 18 inch construction paper
>   Pencil
>   One 36 inch-long piece of thick string or heavy wool in a color to complement construction paper
>   Needle with a large eye
>   12 inch ruler

Directions: Have the class read and carry out these instructions:

1. Fold the construction paper in half with the short sides together (see illustration 1.).
2. Stack the typing paper into one pile.
3. Place one sheet of folded construction paper on the top of the typing paper stack; place the other on the bottom of the pile.
4. With a ruler, mark a line ¾ inch from the open ends of the construction paper.
5. On that line, draw a dot 1 inch from each end.
6. On that same line, draw a dot at the middle and then halfway between the existing dots (see illustration 2.).
7. Have a friend hold the covers and pages firmly.
8. Thread the needle and knot the ends of the string.
9. Begin to sew by pushing the needle through the packet of papers at one of the end dots.
10. At the next dot, poke the needle through the packet of paper, but do not sew through. Pull the needle out. This hole helps to give the location for sewing from the bottom side.
11. Continue to sew back and forth along the row of dots (see illustration 3.).
12. Sew around the back edge of the book and sew to the other end. Pull the thread through each hole three times as the back is sewn.
13. Knot the ends of string at the first sewing hole.
14. Now you have a book in which to write stories or draw pictures.

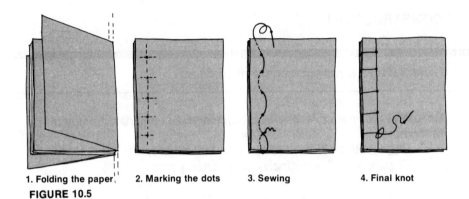

| 1. Folding the paper | 2. Marking the dots | 3. Sewing | 4. Final knot |

FIGURE 10.5

Variation:
Plan other activities from such sources as the following:

What to Do When There's Nothing to Do. Elizabeth M. Gregg. New York: Dell Publishing Co., Inc., 1970.
838 Ways to Amuse a Child. June Johnson. New York: Crown Publishers, Inc., 1988.

BIBLIOTHERAPY

10.6 Read About Others (Primary/Intermediate)

Objective: To promote children's understanding of themselves and others

Materials:
Bulletin board
Appropriate trade books
Set of suggestions, as follows:

1. Share a book that can develop an appreciation of differences and a respect for people who differ from you.
2. Discuss a book about getting along with people of your age.
3. Report on a book about people who are poor.
4. Tell a story that addresses the topic of self-acceptance.
5. Tell how some handicapped person learned to overcome his or her handicap.
6. Share how a book character learned to handle change.

Directions: Post the set of suggestions on the bulletin board. Display books on the table beneath the bulletin board. For example, for the suggestions given above, such books as the following may be displayed:

Beim's *Two is a Team*—primary; Jackson's *Call Me Charley*—
  intermediate (portrays blacks); Armer's *Waterless
  Mountain*—primary; Means' *Whispering Girl*—
  intermediate (portrays Indians).
Carle's *Do you Want to be My Friend*—primary; Yashima's *Crow
  Boy*—intermediate.
Seredy's *A Tree for Peter*—primary; Lenski's *Strawberry
  Girl*—intermediate.
Anderson's *"Ugly Duckling"*—primary; Twain's *Huckleberry Finn*—
  intermediate.

Variation:
  Don't overlook valuable resources, such as:

Bernstein, Joanne E. *Books to Help Children Cope with Separation
  and Loss.* New York: R.R. Bowker, 1983.
Dreyer, Sharon S. The Bookfinder, a Guide to Children's Literature
  About the Needs and Problems of Youth Ages 2–15. 2 volumes.
  Circle Pines, Minnesota: American Guidance Service, 1985.
Tway, Eileen, ed. *Reading Ladders for Human Relations*, Sixth ed.
  Urbana, Illinois: National Council of Teachers of English, 1981.

CURRICULUM AREAS

Relate to Subjects (Primary/Intermediate) **10.7**

Objective: To build children's interest in mathematics curriculum areas
Materials:
  Cards with excerpts from trade books dealing with math
  concepts, as illustrated
  Bulletin board
  Mathematics trade books

Just for Fun Card

Multiply this number by 36: 12345679
Now, what is 12345679 x 9? 18? 27? 45? 54? 63? 72? 81?

Find out your Friend's Age

a. Tell him or her to: Multiply the number of the month in which he or she was born by 100 (Jan. is 1, Feb. 2, etc.)
b. To the product, add the day of the month in which he or she was born.
c. Multiply this sum by 2.
d. Add 9 to the product.
e. Multiply the sum by 5.
f. Add 8 to the product.
g. Multiply the sum by 10.
h. Subtract 419 from the product.
i. To the sum add the age.
j. Give the final result. (When this last number is declared, you subtract 111. The first two digits on the right are the age. The next two digits (third and fourth) from the right are the day of birth. The remaining digits on the left are the month.)

"The Magic Number 4"

Do you know the explanation of this trick?
1. Add 6 to a secret number (1 through 9).
b. Double the new number.
c. Subtract 4.
d. Divide the difference by 2.
e. Now subtract the secret number first selected.

Directions: Post the cards on the bulletin board. Sets of books could be displayed on the table beneath the bulletin board. Various ways of sharing them could be utilized: (a) the books could be read aloud to the children; the (b) children could read on their own and share with the class or a group; (c) committee work could be done by children; and (d) activity or laboratory experiences could be performed by children.

Variations:

Don't overlook the many resources for locating mathematics tradebooks, such as the following:

Teachers editions of children's mathematics textbook series.

Professional textbooks on elementary school mathematics.

Professional texts on children's literature (e.g., Charlotte Huck, *Children's Literature in the Elementary School* 4th ed., New York: Holt Rinehart, and Winston, Inc., 1987.)

Articles (for example: Lucille B. Strain, "Children's Literature: An Aid in Mathematics Instruction," *The Arithmetic Teacher* 16 (October 1969), p. 451–455).

Elementary school librarians.

Series such as the *Franklin Mathematics Series,* available from Rand McNally Publishing Co., P. O. Box 7600, Chicago, IL 60680; *Crowell Young Mathematics Books,* Thomas Y. Crowell, 665 5th Ave. New York, NY 10022; and *Holt Wise Owl Books,* available from Holt, Rinehart, and Winston, Inc., 383 Madison Ave. New York, NY 10017.

Clarence E. Hardgrove and Herbert F. Miller, *Mathematics Library—Elementary and Junior High School,* 3rd ed., Washington, D.C.: National Council of Teachers of Mathematics, 1973.

Some mathematics concept books, appropriate for grades 4–8, follow:

NUMERATION
Adler, Irving, *Numerals: New Dresses for Old Numbers.* New York: John Day, 1964.
Asimov, Isaac, *Realm of Numbers.* Boston: Houghton Mifflin, 1966.
Selfridge, Oliver, *Fingers Come in Fives.* Boston: Houghton Mifflin, 1966.

ADDITION
Rossetti, Christina, *Adding: A Poem* (Young Owl Books). New York: Holt, Rinehart, and Winston, 1968.

SUBTRACTION
Whitney, David, *Let's Find Out About Subtraction.* New York: Franklin Watts, 1968.

MULTIPLICATION
Trivett, John, *Building Tables on Tables.* New York: T. Y. Crowell, 1976.
Whitney, David, *Easy Book of Multiplication.* New York: Franklin Watts, 1969.
Zim, Herbert S. *Codes and Secret Writing.* New York: Morrow, 1948.

FRACTIONS
Bell, Thelma, *Snow.* New York: The Viking Press, 1954.
Dennis, J. Richard, *Fractions Are a Part of Things.* New York: Thomas Y. Crowell, 1973.

GEOMETRY
Bendick, Jeanne, *Take Shapes, Lines and Letters.* New York: McGraw, 1962.
Ellisa, Else, *Fun with Lines and Curves.* New York: Lathrop, 1972.

Hoban, Tana, *Shapes and Things*. New York: Macmillan, 1970.
Phillips, Jo, *Right Angles: Paper-folding Geometry*. New York: Crowell, 1972.
Sitomer, Mindel, *What is Symmetry?* New York: Crowell, 1970.
Sitomer, Mindel, *Lines, Segments, Polygons*. New York: Crowell, 1972.

MEASUREMENT
Adler, Irving, *Time In Your Life*. New York: John Day, 1955.
Bendick, Jeanne, *How Much and How Many: The Story of Weights and Measures*. New York: Whittlesey House, 1947.
Branley, Franklyn, *Think Metric!* New York: Crowell, 1972.
Dripdale, Thomas and John Dunworth, *Millions of People* (Wise Owl Books). New York: Holt, 1965.
Epstein, Beryl and Sam Epstein, *The First Book of Measurement*. New York: Watts, 1960.
Evenson, A. E., *About the History of the Calendar*. Chicago: Children's Press, 1972.
Pine, Tillie S., and Joseph Levine, *Measurements and How We Use Them*. New York: McGraw-Hill, 1974.
Reinfeld, Fred, *The Story of Civil War Money*. New York: Sterling, 1959.
Strivastava, Jane, *Area*. New York: Crowell, 1974.
Strivastava, Jane, *Weighing and Balancing*. New York: Crowell, 1970.

NUMBER THEORY
Lerch, Harold, *Numbers in the Land of Hand*. Carbondale, Illinois: Southern Illinois University Press, 1966.
O'Brien, Thomas C., *Odds and Evens*. New York: Crowell, 1971.

FUNCTION/STATISTICS/PROBABILITIES
Linn, Charles F., *Probability*. New York: Crowell, 1972.
Papy, Frederique, *Graph Games*. New York: Crowell, 1971.
Strivastava, Jane Jonas, *Statistics*. New York: Crowell, 1973.

MATH PEOPLE
Stonaker, Frances Benson, *Famous Mathematicians*. Philadelphia: Lippincott, 1966.

OTHER
Tannenbaum, Beulah, and Myra Stillman, *Understanding Maps*. New York: McGraw-Hill, 1969.
Norman, Gertrude, *The First Book of Music*. New York: Watts, 1954.

Barr, George, *Entertaining With Number Tricks*. New York: McGraw Hill, 1971.
Fletcher, Helen Hill, *Puzzles and Quizzes*. New York: Abelard-Schuman, 1971.
Golick, Margie, *Deal Me In!* New York: Norton Publishers, 1973.
Linn, Charles F., *Puzzles, Patterns, and Pasttimes*. New York: Doubleday, 1969.
Simon, Lemark, *The Day the Numbers Disappeared*. New York: McGraw-Hill, 1963.

There are poems that have mathematics as a topic, such as the following:

Barnstone, Aliki, "Numbers," in *The Real Tin Flower*. New York: Crowell-Collier, 1968.
Brown, Beatrice Curtis, "Jonathan Bing Does Arithmetic," in *Gaily We Parade,* edited by John E. Brewton. New York: Macmillan Co., 1964.
Read, Sir Herbert, "Equations," in *Catch Me a Wind,* edited by Patricia Hubbell. New York: Atheneum Publishers, 1968.
Sandburg, Carl, "Arithmetic," in *Wind Song*. New York: Harcourt, Brace and World, 1960.
"There Was An Old Man Who Said Do" (Anonymous), in *Rainbow in the Sky,* edited by L. Untermeyer. New York: Harcourt, Brace, and World, 1935.

REAL LIFE READING

Tie A Clove Hitch (Primary/Intermediate)   **10.8**

Objective: To help students with reading a set of directions such as found in scout handbooks, hobby and game directions, repair manuals, nature guides, and the like
Materials:
Rope
Post

FIGURE 10.8

Directions:
1. Take one end of the rope in your right hand. With your left hand, hold the rest of the rope across the front of the post.
2. Pass the end of the rope around in back of the post.
3. Bring it around to the front of the post. Cross it over the long part, making an X. Hold the X with left thumb and forefinger.

4. Pass the rope to the right again, wrapping it around the post *below* the first turn.
5. Push the rope end under the X, going from left to right so that it comes out between the two turns around the post.
6. Pull the short end to the right, the long end to the left. As long as there is a steady pull on the long end, the hitch will not loosen.
7. Untie or loosen by pushing both ends toward the center.
8. Check illustration for accuracy.

Variations:

1. Directions for "Whipping a Rope" or "Hanking a Rope" may be used.
2. Directions for various types of knots and hitches, such as square knot, sheet bend, or bowline, may be used.
3. Directions for various types of lashing, such as square lashing, sheer lashing, continuous lashing, may be used.
4. Directions from other hobby and game books, repair manuals, and the like may be used.

Read a Menu (Primary/Intermediate)   **10.9**

Objective: To provide children with practice reading a sample menu
Materials:
   A sample (or real) menu such as on page 194.
Directions: After presenting the menu, question the class about it, asking such things as:
   What is the price of a beverage?
   Can chili be ordered separately? If so, what is the heading under which it is found?
   What else do you get when you order a sirloin steak?
   How many desserts are listed?
Variation:
   The same type of activity may be prepared for related types of materials, such as a TV guide, a telephone book, a catalogue, a cereal box, and food or medicine containers, such as milk cartons, cough drop boxes, and aspirin bottles.

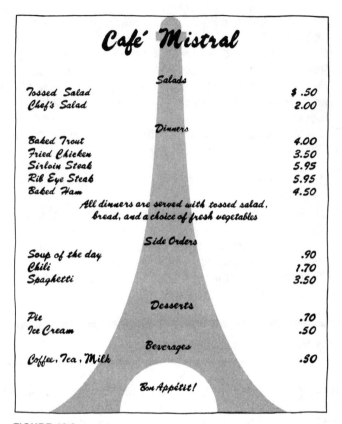

FIGURE 10.9

10.10 Read a Sports Card (Primary/Intermediate)

Objective: To provide practice in reading sample sports cards
Materials:

A sample sports card as illustrated

Set of questions, as follows:

How tall is Bobby Orr?

What is Orr's total points in his playing career?

What award did Bobby Orr receive several times?

For which professional hockey teams has Orr played?

Why did Orr play so little in 1976–77?

For how many years has Orr played professional hockey?

Bobby Orr, Defenseman, Black Hawks				
Ht.: 6'0"		Wt.: 200		
Age: 29		Years Pro: 11		
Scoring Record	Games Played	Goals	Assists	Points
Career	651	268	643	911
1976–77	20	4	19	23

Regarded by most as greatest player in the game. Revolutionized the game as a rushing defenseman. Won more individual awards than any player in hockey history. Born March 20, 1948, in Parry Sound, Ontario, Canada. Joined the Boston Bruins at 18. Won Norris Trophy as league's outstanding defenseman for eight straight years. Limited to 20 games last season after fifth knee operation. Shy, private person who shuns personal attention. Signed by the Chicago Black Hawks for $3-million as free agent after ten glorious seasons with Boston.

Directions: After presenting the sample card, ask the questions and discuss the answers.

Variation:

The same type of activity may be prepared for related types of materials, such as stamp collection journals, greeting cards, calendars, travel brochures, and report cards.

Maintain Your Bicycle (Primary/Intermediate) 10.11

Objective: To provide practice reading owner's handbooks

Material:

Sample passage from an owner's handbook, such as the following example:

Fixing a Flat Bicycle Tire

Riding on very soft tires or riding when the tire and tube are punctured, will cause damage to the tire and the tube. A flat tire (if the puncture in the tube was caused by a nail) can often be fixed by patching and without having to remove the wheel from the bicycle.

Patching

1. If you can visually locate the nail hole in the tire, mark the area.
2. Using a small screwdriver or the top of a key, press the valve-core plunger in and hold it in until all air empties from the tube—use hand pressure to squeeze the tire flat to get all the air out.

3. Using your fingers, pry one edge of the tire off the rim along the puncture-marked area, then pull out the tube so you can work on it. Do not use screwdrivers or other sharp objects to pry off the tire, as you might damage the tube.

4. Read the following instructions supplied in the tube patching kit (usually a tube or rubber patch cement, several rubber patches, and a scraper or buffer are provided).

   a. Use the scraper to roughen the tube at the puncture.

   b. Apply a coating of rubber cement to the area around the puncture, and allow it to dry completely.

   c. Peel off the cloth from the rubber patch, and press the patch to the tube surface where you have applied the cement. Press firmly.

   d. Carefully fit the tube into the tire (making sure it is not twisted) and then fit the tire (using fingers only) onto the rim. Be sure the tire is seated evenly by checking the embossed guide line on the tire.

   e. Be sure the valve stem is straight up before you begin pumping air into the tire.

   f. Carefully pump up the tire with a few pump strokes, and check the guide line to ensure correct seating in the rim. If the line is even, pump up the tire to the required pressure.

   g. Then apply a little water to your finger tip and place it in the center of the valve stem. If the water forms an air bubble it indicates air is escaping. Tighten the valve core, and repeat the water test. If it forms a bubble, the valve is defective and must be replaced.

Set of sample questions, as follows:

What happens when you press the valve core plunger in?

Why should you not use a sharp object to pry off the tire?

What items are usually found in a tube patching kit?

How can you be sure the tire is seated evenly when replaced?

How do you determine if air is escaping from the tire?

Directions: After students have read the directions, discuss the questions with them.

Variations:

1. Use directions for removing wheels.
2. Use other handbooks for other items, particularly assembling, operation, adjustment, and maintenance instructions.

Easy Reading Book Series

1. Adapted Classics. New York: Globe Book Company.
   47 titles, including the following:

Book	Reading Level
The Prince and the Pauper	4–5
Robin Hood	4–5
Swiss Family Robinson	4–5
Tales Worth Retelling	5–6
Tom Sawyer	4–5
Treasure Island	5–6
Western Stories of Bret Harte	5–6

2. American Adventure Series, edited by Emmett A. Betts. New York: Harper & Row.
   22 titles, 2nd through 6th grade reading levels, including the following:

Book	Reading Level
Squanto and the Pilgrims	2
Chief Black Hawk	3
Alaska Bush Pilot	4
Rocket Pioneer	5
John Paul Jones	6

3. American Heritage Series. New York: American Book Company. Grades 5–6.
4. Americans All Series. San Francisco, CA: Field Educational Publications Grades 4–5.
5. Animal Adventure Series. Westchester, IL: Benefic Press. Preprimer to grade 1.
6. Basic Vocabulary Series. Champaign, IL: Garrard. Grade 2.
7. Beginner Books. New York: Random House. Grades 1–2. Titles include the following:

Book	Reading Level
The Cat in the Hat	2.1
Bennett Cerf's Book of Riddles	2.2
Green Eggs and Ham	1.9
Hop on Pop	1.7

8. Better Reading Series, by John F. Rambeau and Nancy Rambeau. Oklahoma City: Educational Guidelines Co. (Division of The Economy Co.). Grades 2–6.
9. Blackberry Farm Books. New York: McKay. Grades K–2.
10. Box Car Children's Books, by Gertrude Warner, Glenview, IL: Scott, Foresman. Grade 3.
11. Butternut Bill Series, by Edith McCall. Westchester, IL: Benefic Press. Preprimer–1.
12. Button Family Adventure Series, by Edith McCall. Westchester, IL: Benefic Press. Preprimer–3.
13. Checkered Flag Series, by Henry A. Bamman and Robert J. Whitehead. San Francisco: Field Educational Publications. Grades 2–4.
14. Childhood of Famous Americans Series. Indianapolis: Bobbs-Merrill. Grade 4.
15. Clyde Bulla Books. New York: Crowell. Grade 3.
16. Cowboy Sam Series, by Edna Walker Chandler. Westchester, IL: Benefic Press. Preprimer–3.
17. Curriculum Motivation Series, Chicago, IL: Rand McNally. Grades 1–3.

18. Dan Frontier Series, by William J. Hurley. Westchester, IL: Benefic Press, Preprimer–4.
19. Deep Sea Adventure Series, by James C. Coleman, Frances Berres, William C. Briscoe, and Frank M. Hewett. San Francisco: Field Educational Publications. Grades 1–5.
20. Discovery Books Series. Champaign, IL: Garrard. Grade 3.
21. Easy Reading Picture Story Books. Chicago, IL: Children's Press. Grades 1–3. Titles include the following:

Book	Reading Level
Martin Luther King, Jr.	1
Seven Diving Ducks	2
True Book of Dinosaurs	3

22. Easy-to-Read Series, by Sarah Derman. Westchester, IL: Benefic Press. Preprimer–1.
23. Everyreader Library. New York: Webster Division of McGraw-Hill. Grades 4–5.
24. Fairy Tales of Many Lands. New York: Dutton. Grades 1–4.
25. Field Literature Program, K–6, by Henry Bamman, Helen Huus, and Robert Whitehead. Palo Alto, CA: Field Educational Publications. Preprimer–6.
26. First Reading Books. Champaign, IL: Garrard. Grade 1.
27. Folk and Fairy Tales Series. Columbus, OH: Merrill. Grades 1–4.
28. Folklore of the World, Champaign, IL: Garrard. Grade 3.
29. Follett Just Beginning-to-Read Books, by Margaret Hillert. Chicago, IL: Follett. Preprimer level.
30. Follet Beginning-to-Read Books. Chicago, IL: Follet. Grades 1–2.
31. Frontiers of America Books, by Edith McCall. Chicago, IL: Children's Press. Grade 3.
32. Gateway Books. New York: Random House. Grades 2–3.
33. Golden Rule Series. New York: American Book Company. Grades 1–6.
34. Happenings, by Mary W. Sullivan. San Francisco, CA: Field Educational Publications. Grade 4.
35. Indians of America Books. Chicago, IL: Children's Press. Grades 2–4.
36. Instant Readers, by Bill Martin and Peggy Brogan. New York: Holt, Rinehart and Winston. Primary grades.
37. Interesting Reading Series. Chicago, IL: Follett. Grades 3–4.
38. Jerry Series, by Florence Battle. Westchester, IL: Benefic Press. Preprimer–grade 3.
39. Jim Forest Readers, by John F. Rambeau and Nancy Rambeau. San Francisco: Field Educational Publications. Grades 1–3.

40. Junior Everyreader Series. New York: Webster Division of McGraw-Hill. Grades 2–4.
41. Modern Adventure Series. New York: Harper & Row. Grades 4–6.
42. Morgan Bay Mystery Series, by John Rambeau and Nancy Rambeau. San Francisco: Field Educational Publications. Grades 2–4.
43. New Easy-to-Read Books. New York: Random House. Grades 3–6.
44. Our Animal Story Books. Lexington, MA: Heath. Preprimer.
45. Owl Books, Bill Martin, ed. New York: Holt, Rinehart and Winston. Grades K–6.
46. Pioneer Series. Westchester, IL: Benefic Press. Grade 3.
47. Piper Books, Boston: Houghton Mifflin. Intermediate grades. Titles include the following:
    Sam Houston: Friend of the Indians
    Abigail Adams: The President's Lady
48. Pleasure Reading Series. Champaign, IL: Garrard. Grade 4.
49. Putnam's Sports Series. New York: Putnam's. Grades 3–6.
50. Racing Wheels Readers, by Anabel Dean. Westchester, IL: Benefic Press. Grades 2–4.
51. Raggedy Ann Series. Indianapolis: Bobbs-Merrill. Grades 4–8.
52. Read-by-Yourself Books. Boston: Houghton Mifflin. Primer–2.
53. Read for Fun Series. New York: Webster Division of McGraw-Hill. Grades 1–3.
54. Read It Myself Books. New York: American Book Company. Grades 1–3.
55. Reading Adventure Series. Columbus, OH: Merrill. Grade 4.
56. Reading Incentive Program. Glendale, CA: Bowmar. Grade 4.
57. Reading Literature Series. Columbus, OH: Merrill. Grades 1–6.
58. Reading Today Series. Indianapolis: Bobbs-Merrill. Grades 4–6.
59. Sailor Jack Series, by Selma Wassermann and Jack Wassermann. Westchester, IL: Benefic Press. Preprimer–3.
60. Shapes Around Us Reading Series, by Frances Fox and Penrod Moss. San Francisco: Century Communications, Inc. Primary reading levels.
61. Simplified Classics, Glenview, IL: Scott, Foresman. Grades 4–6. Titles include the following:
    Around the World in Eighty Days
    Call of the Wild
    Famous Mysteries
    Tom Sawyer
    Treasure Island

62. Space Age Books, by Hazel W. Carson. Westchester, IL: Benefic Press. Grades 2–3.
63. Space Science Fiction Series, by Henry A. Bamman et al. Westchester, IL: Benefic Press. Grades 2–6.
64. Sports Mystery Series, by Evelyn Lunemann. Westchester, IL: Benefic Press, Grades 2–4.
65. Step-Up Books. New York: Random House. Grades 2–3.
66. Superstars, Creative Education Books, by James J. Olsen. Chicago, IL: Children's Press. Grades 3–6.
67. Target Books. Champaign, IL: Garrard. Grades 3–4.
68. Target Today Series, by Charles Brown, Helen Truher, and Phillip Wiese. Westchester, IL: Benefic Press. Grades 1–4.
69. Time Machine Series, by Gene Darby. San Francisco: Field Educational Publications. Preprimer–grade 2.
70. Time to Read Series. Philadelphia, PA: Lippincott. Grades 1–6.
71. Tom Logan Series, by Edna Walker Chandler. Westchester, IL: Benefic Press. Preprimer–3.
72. Treasure Chest of Good Reading Stories. Indianapolis: Bobbs-Merrill. Grades 4–6.
73. Treasury of Literature Readers, Columbus, OH: Merrill. Grades 3–6.
74. Treat Truck Series, by Genevieve Gray, Sylvajean Harrington, Lee Harrington, and Sandra Altheide. Westchester, IL: Benefic Press. Preprimer–3.
75. Venture Books, Champaign, IL: Garrard. Grades 1–2.
76. Wildlife Adventure Series, by Rhoda Leonard and William S. Briscoe. San Francisco: Field Educational Publications. Grades 2–4.
77. Wonder Story Books, by Miriam Huber and Mabel O'Donnell. New York: Harper & Row. Primer–3.
78. World of Adventure Series, by Henry A. Bamman and Robert Whitehead. Westchester, IL: Benefic Press. Grades 2–6.
79. Yearling Individualized Reading Program. New York: Noble and Noble. Grades 3–6.
80. Young Heroes Library Series. New York: Lantern Press. Grades 4–8.
81. Young Readers Bookshelf Series. New York: Lantern Press. Grades 4–8.

appendix b

Multilevel Instructional Materials

Advanced Reading Skills Series, Grades 3–6. St. Louis, Missouri: Milliken.

Be A Better Reader, Books 1–4, by Nila B. Smith. Englewood Cliffs, NJ: Prentice-Hall.

Bracken Specific Reading Skills Program, Grades 1–8. Dallas: Jones-Kenilworth Co.

Califone Remedial Reading Program, Levels 1–9, Los Angeles, CA: Rheem Califone.

Controlled Reader Sets A–F, Levels 1–6. Huntington, New York: Educational Developmental Laboratories, a division of McGraw-Hill.

EDL Study Skills Library, Levels 3–9. Huntington, New York: Educational Developmental Laboratories, a division of McGraw-Hill.

Gates-Peardon Reading Exercises, Grades 2–6. New York: Teacher's College Press.

Kaleidoscope of Skills: Reading, Grades 5–7. Chicago: Science Research Associates.

Macmillan Reading Spectrum, by J. S. Weinberg et al. New York: Macmillan.

McCall-Crabbs Standard Test Lessons in Reading, Grades 3–7. New York: Teacher's College Press.

M.C.P. New Phonics Workbooks, A, B, C. Cleveland, OH: Modern Curriculum Press.

Merrill Phonics Skilltext Series: The Sound and Structure of Words, Grades 1–6, by Josephine B. Wolfe. Columbus, OH: Merrill.

Multiple Skills Series, Levels 4–9, by Richard A Boning. New York: Lowell and Linwood, Ltd.

New Diagnostic Reading Workbook Series, Grades 1–6, by Eleanor M. Johnson. Columbus, OH: Charles E. Merrill.

The New Practice Readers, Grades 2–6. Manchester, MO: Webster Division, McGraw-Hill.

The New Specific Skills Series, Levels 1–12, by R. A. Boning. Baldwin, NY: Barnell Loft.

Patterns, Sounds, and Meaning, Levels 1–4. Boston: Allyn and Bacon.

Phonics Crossword Puzzles, Levels 1–6. Cincinnati, OH: McCormick-Mathers.

Reader's Digest Reading Skill Builders, Grades 1–6. Pleasantville, N.Y.: Educational Division, Reader's Digest.

Reader's Digest Science Reader, Grades 4–6. Pleasantville, N.Y.: Reader's Digest.

Reading Comprehension, Grades 3–8, by Jane Ervin. Cambridge, MA: Educators Publishing.

Reading Development Kits, Grades 1–10, Menlo Park, CA: Addison-Wesley.

Reading for Concepts, Grades 1–6, by William Liddle. New York: McGraw-Hill.

Reading for Meaning, Rev. Ed., Grades 4–6, by John H. Coleman and Ann Jungeblut. Philadelphia: Lippincott.

Reading for Understanding, Junior Ed., Grades 3–8, Chicago: Science Research Associates.

Reading Skill Texts, Grades PP–6, by Murray Anderson et al. Columbus, OH: Charles E. Merrill.

Science Research Associates Reading Laboratories, Levels I, Ia, Ib, Ic, IIa, IIb, IIc, IIIa, IIIb, IVa. Chicago: Science Research Associates.

Skilpacers, Elementary through junior high. New York: Random House.

Supportive Reading Skills Series, Levels 1–6 and Advanced by Richard A. Boning. New York: Dexter and Westbrook, Ltd.

subject–skill index of activities

206 Subject-Skill Index of Activities